Representation of Disability in Children's Video Games

D1784229

Representation of Disability in Children's Video Games looks at how children's engagement with characters and stories in video games helps create the perception of disability they have as teens and adults. Drawing on child development theory supported by neuroscience, the book shows how the scaffold of information, the schema, adults have of disability is first created at a very young age as they interact through play with characters with disabilities in narrative video games.

Positing that early video game play experiences should provide exposure to narrative schemas that add understanding and help create meaning about the disability represented, the book presents how such representation in children's video games maps against cognitive development and the psychomotor and cognitive needs and abilities of children 3–12. Through close readings of over 40 PEGI 3 and PEGI 7 (ESRB E, 10+) games and analysis of games as diverse as *Backyard Baseball and Sly Cooper*, the author defines broad categories of representation: representation as cosmetic, providing exposure but not game play utility; as incidental, used as a device that provides purpose for the narrative; or as more authentically representing the disability as integral to the character and their life. The book provides readers with an overview of contemporary games that betters their understanding of how children's games present disability and how children create their perceptions through interaction with characters and stories.

This book will be of interest to academics and students of game studies in topics such as behavioural science, ethics, and HCI, as well as in sociology, communications, and digital media. It is pertinent in particular to game developers and to educators, disability advocates, parents, and policy makers.

Krystina Madej researched children's narrative games at Georgia Tech in Atlanta, Georgia for ten years and currently holds a Research Professorship in The Centre for Games and Animation at the University of Lower Silesia in Wroclaw, Poland.

Routledge Research in Disability and Media Studies

Katie Ellis, Curtin University

Disability and Digital Television Cultures
Katie Ellis

Disability, Media, and Representations: Other Bodies
Edited by Jacob Johanssen and Diana Garrisi

Gaming Disability
Disability Perspectives on Contemporary Video Games
Edited by Katie Ellis, Tama Leaver, and Mike Kent

Disabled People Transforming Media Culture for a More Inclusive World
Beth A. Haller

Representation of Disability in Children's Video Games
Krystina Madej

For more information about this series, please visit: https://www.routledge.com/ Routledge-Research-in-Disability-and-Media-Studies/book-series/RRDMS

Representation of Disability in Children's Video Games

By Krystina Madej

Routledge
Taylor & Francis Group

LONDON AND NEW YORK

First published 2024
by Routledge
4 Park Square, Milton Park, Abingdon, Oxon OX14 4RN

and by Routledge
605 Third Avenue, New York, NY 10158

Routledge is an imprint of the Taylor & Francis Group, an informa business

© 2024 Krystina Madej

British Library Cataloguing-in-Publication Data
A catalogue record for this book is available from the British Library

Library of Congress Cataloging-in-Publication Data
Names: Madej, Krystina, author.
Title: Representation of disability in children's video games /
by Krystina Madej.
Description: Abingdon, Oxon ; New York, NY : Routledge, 2024. |
Series: Routledge research in disability and media studies |
Includes bibliographical references and index.
Identifiers: LCCN 2023047609 (print) | LCCN 2023047610 (ebook) |
ISBN 9781032553887 (hardback) | ISBN 9781032553894 (paperback) |
ISBN 9781003430445 (ebook)
Subjects: LCSH: People with disabilities in video games. |
Video games andchildren. | Child development.
Classification: LCC GV1469.34.H36 M34 2024 (print) |
LCC GV1469.34.H36 (ebook) | DDC 794.8/4527--dc23/eng/20231122
LC record available at https://lccn.loc.gov/2023047609
LC ebook record available at https://lccn.loc.gov/2023047610

ISBN: 978-1-032-55388-7 (hbk)
ISBN: 978-1-032-55389-4 (pbk)
ISBN: 978-1-003-43044-5 (ebk)

DOI: 10.4324/9781003430445

Typeset in Times New Roman
by KnowledgeWorks Global Ltd.

For Jan Stasieńko, defender of inclusion, for his generosity of spirit and for sharing his work, home, and family. Never were video games more enthusiastically embraced than by Szymon, Lukasz, and Pola under the tolerant but critical eye of Aga Dytman-Stasieńko. And for my own trio of gamers, Nicola, Michael, and Daniel, who brought home a constant stream of new games to be played and critiqued.

Contents

Acknowledgements

This book is based in part on the research conducted for the project "Fragile Avatars? Representations of disability in video games, in linguistic, visual, narrative, and structural context," headed by Jan Stasieńko, Director of Research in Media and Communications at the University of Lower Silesia, Wrocław, Poland. The project was funded by The State Fund for Rehabilitation of Disabled People (PFRON) under the agreement number BEA/000057/BFD. "Fragile Avatars," the resulting publication, with authors Jan Stasieńko, Agnieszka Dytman-Stasieńko, Krystina Madej, Adam Flamma, and Maciej Śledź, is licensed under a Creative Commons Attribution (CC-BY) 4.0 License that allows authors and others to share the work with an acknowledgment of the work's authorship and initial publication.

1 Introduction

Lennie: A New Way to Think of Disability

A Without Prejudice View

In 1995, Geoffrey the Giraffe, mascot to the popular retailer *Toys R Us*, was the third most recognized animation character in the US. When the company released the video game *Geoffrey Goes to the Fair* as one of its Christmas offerings in 1998, it had 800 stores nationally and its audience consisted of a large segment of kids aged 3–10 across the US.

Why do I introduce you to *Geoffrey Goes to the Fair*? Geoffrey's group of friends in the game are a diverse bunch and among them is Lennie the Lion. Lennie uses a wheelchair. He's one of the first characters in a children's commercial video game to do so. In the opening scene of the game, Geoffrey and his friends race down the street towards the audience. Bicycles and wheelchairs race forward and fall back as each of the kids vies to get ahead. Geoffrey and Lennie are often head-to-head and wheel-to-wheel. The kids' faces glow with excitement. A quick zoom to the wheels shows that these turn as fast on the wheelchair as on the bicycles next to it.

Lennie is on equal footing (wheeling) with his friends. He's one of the gang. Throughout the game he is part of every crowd scene, he doesn't get any special treatment, and he isn't shown to have a disadvantage. He's just an average kid, like the others, having a fun day at the fair. Millions of children, many of whom had never seen a wheelchair previously, were introduced to a new animated friend who happened to use a wheelchair. They got to interact with Lennie in an everyday environment and did everyday things with him and his friends. In an era when positive representation of disability was scant, Lennie introduced an entire generation of children to a "without prejudice" view of disability that was radical and precedent setting.

How Did the Game Come About?

From 1966, Geoffrey, his kid helpers, and sometimes his giraffe family, featured in print, radio, and TV ads for *Toys R Us*. The memorable song "I don't want to

DOI: 10.4324/9781003430445-1

grow up, I'm a *Toys R Us* kid" expressed the sentiment of the age. The children depicted in most of the ads were toddlers, preschoolers, and k–2, approximately aged 3–7. *Geoffrey Goes to the Fair* was released for Christmas 1998. It was developed by Apptastic, a small software company that normally provided *Toys R Us* with proprietary quote software. Because the company also created animations for ads, Warren Pratte and his partners, Dave Stephenson and Darryl Wizenberg, decided to approach *Toys R Us* with a proposal for a 3D adventure children's game. There was hesitation from company management at first, but because the relationship between the companies was excellent, Apptastic was told to go ahead. With surprisingly little direction or oversight and no requirement to promote the store, the game became an open-ended opportunity.

With Apptastic, "diversity" got lucky. The development team included Greg Burke, who was an elementary school teacher of children with special needs, and Warren Pratte's brother, Dave, who was writing his PhD on prejudice against minorities. The development team saw an opportunity to design characters with diversity at a time when games were overwhelmingly populated by white males. It made a conscious choice to include three female friends, three male friends, and a friend with a mobility disability who uses a wheelchair. Just representation wasn't enough for the team, it wanted "thoughtful" representation for two reasons, reaffirmation for children with disabilities who played the game and a positive experience of disability for children who did not have disabilities. To this effect they intended to create a perception of equality among Geoffrey and his friends. With Lennie in a wheelchair, how did they plan to accomplish this? They did so by not making Lennie other. He is not a sufferer, he does need a cure, he does not need improving. The wheelchair is not Lennie's defining characteristic, its use is not given a back story, there is no dialogue about it; the persona of the Lion, King of the Jungle, bespeaks strength; from the first scene, the balance is tipped towards equality with characters racing towards the audience and Lennie surging forward and falling back as equally capable.

The production team wanted to create a seamless experience so that at no point would players experience Lennie's movements as awkward or unnatural. As production progressed, they realized different rigging had to be created for Lennie because wheelchair movements were not standard. The team had built the park before they realized that slopes and accessibility would need to be adjusted to accommodate wheelchair requirements according to the best practices of the day. With this new awareness, curbs were identified, arcade tabletops lowered, and ramps added to the stair access to the stage and haunted house. While these additions were not necessarily reflective of reality at the time (ramps, for instance, were not available in most places), they had the advantage of presenting Lennie's actions as a more constituent part of the friend's park experience.

The team also wanted to make the game more accessible to younger children (3 or 4). They added three levels of play difficulty, audio and image cues, and easier mechanics. They considered that because young children's fine motor skills are only developing, some would find it hard to use a mouse to move a car in a direction and at the same time click the mouse for action. With the new mechanics, rather than moving cars along with the mouse, children could point to where bumper cars were supposed to arrive to provide a trajectory for movement.[1] These features helped make the game more accessible for all players not just younger children. Apptastic did progressive testing during which children were interviewed individually by designers. Suggestions were incorporated and there was a second testing during which children would note, "Oh you fixed that." When the game was released, the company received many calls from organizations that represented people with disabilities, asking "Why don't you have a character who is hearing impaired, or visually impaired, or …." Apptastic had not added Lennie to make a statement about disabilities. Lennie was not a symbol, he was, as are all people with disabilities, just part of daily life.

Lennie in his wheelchair provided a positive view of disability to a generation of children at a time when public perception in the US was changing. Until 1974, less than 25 years earlier, a number of cities in the US (including Chicago and San Francisco) were just changing laws they had that targeted poor and disabled people. It had been illegal for "any person, who is diseased, maimed, mutilated or deformed in any way, so as to be an unsightly or disgusting object, to expose himself or herself to public view" (Schweik, 2009, p. 293). It was not until the *Americans with Disabilities Act of 1990* that "public accommodations and commercial facilities" were required to be "readily accessible to and usable by individuals with disabilities" (Cahill, 1995). The game scenarios in *Geoffrey Goes to the Fair* in which Lennie, a wheelchair user, was not being singled out as disabled and was friendly, competent, and competitive, provided a much-needed, well-considered representation of disability.[2]

Background

Since the late 1990s I have undertaken research into children's stories in print and video games and how these correlate with child development. A basic premise I've arrived at for my work in narrative and games is that the schemas children form at a young age are foundational to the perceptions they hold as adults.

When my colleague Jan Stasieńko, Director of Research in Media and Communications at the University of Lower Silesia (ULS), Wroclaw, Poland, was putting together a team to look at the representation of disability in games for a project funded by The State Fund for Rehabilitation of Disabled People, my work in story, children's games, and child development appeared a good match for looking at games for children. Stasieńko has been at the forefront of including individuals with disabilities in research in games. In 2015 he received the "Wroclaw Without Barriers" award from the City Council/the

Municipality of Wroclaw for the scientific project "People with Disabilities as Actors In Motion Capture Sessions." His understanding of disability issues and dedication to research in the area would provide the support I needed to become involved in a study area new to me.

My research for ULS resulted in the chapter "PEGI 3 and PEGI 7 games, representation of disability and children's cognitive development" in the report "Fragile Avatars: Representation of Disability in Video Games" published by ULS in 2021.[3] The chapter tackles something not done previously, it maps games against child development to provide insight into how perception is established at an early age.[4]

This book uses much of that chapter's content and enlarges on it. It supplements existing subject matter and adds new points to consider within the context of the original research. Research on child development and games is presented against a broad understanding of issues surrounding disability, accessibility, and representation in video games gained through online research of these resources, not personal experience. There are many social, political, and academic discussions which address issues of accessibility and cultural attitudes towards people with disabilities in both formal venues (books, academic articles) and social media venues (blogs, newsfeeds). Citations supporting the discussion in this and subsequent chapters are from across all these sources, not only academic ones. Where possible, the original source of quotations is provided, although admittedly, following information through social media to find an authentic and authoritative source is occasionally challenging. The purpose of the book is to provide an opening gambit in creating a knowledge base of child development as it relates to representation in children's games. The information is first for use in academic scholarship and then to provide game developers a nuanced understanding of the affect of their representations and basic facts about how what children are seeing in the games they play constructs their perception so that when they consider adding representation of disability to their games they do so thoughtfully. Finally, and equally importantly, the book is intended to give parents, educators, and policy makers the knowledge for more informed decision-making by detailing how the games children play at a young age help develop perceptions that are basic to their views as adults. The book is written in a narrative style to make the research accessible to all potentially influential audiences to help them make change. There are certainly concerns addressed only lightly or unevenly, or perhaps not at all. I encourage others to fill the gaps.

Context

With the emergence of each new communication technology used to provide information, education, or entertainment, there have been groups of people who have been excluded from using that media because different capabilities made it inaccessible to them. The World Health Organization (WHO) reports that 16% of the world population or 1.6 billion people live with a disability. A 2020 study of over 3,000 players 16–50 in the UK and the US showed 29% and 31%, respectively, who self-identified as having a disability, with mental health being most reported. WHO identifies capabilities in their International Classification of Functioning (ICF) as including vision, hearing and speech communication, mobility, and cognition and learning skills. It considers that individuals, whatever their capability, have a right to be fully and equally participating citizens in society.[5] Our current social model reflects this as a global goal, not yet a reality: it *looks to* accommodate people living with different capabilities rather than to change them to accommodate society. Practically, achieving this goal requires cultural changes in perception of disability as well as creation of accommodation. Sometimes cultural changes need to precede change in accommodation. Sometimes it is necessary to make physical changes that in turn will create awareness and shift cultural perception.

Within a global context, cultures and their encompassing societies take on the challenge of making and enforcing changes. As countries have become more culturally diverse, differences in attitudes make change for the common good difficult. Underlying the difficulty is the inherited meaning of the words we use which are imbued with centuries of cultural understanding and bias (Bakhtin, 1982). The words introduced by WHO, "different capabilities," are, as much as they can be, neutral. The more regularly used word, disability, is not neutral. It was not used in its current context until the 20th century; it now reflects the common view that "a problem exists in a person's body" which limits them and needs to be corrected. It is, rather than the actual impairment or disorder (description of the body or mind), a construct created through "the restriction of activity caused by a contemporary social organization" (Goering, 2015, p. 135), that is, it is the external perception that this impairment is a problem that makes for disability. While impairment may require the assistance of physical aids, disability requires a change in perception that, unfortunately, is long in coming (Goering, 2015; Oliver, 1996). Even though the medical model of disability, which sees disability as an individual's problem with a need for medical attention as the root cause for any disadvantages experienced in living, was discarded in the 1970s, it persists in the media and in games. Language that links disability with suffering and a hope for a cure, and games in which disability is compensated by superpowers, undermine changes in perception (Goering, 2015; Mental Health and Disabilities, 2018). While the disability rights movement has made gains, these "are still fragile and partial" (Switzer, 2003) and it will take much more time than hoped for to undo the "segregation, stigmatization, and discrimination on the basis of disability" that has existed for centuries (Blanck, 2019, p. 605).

Accessibility

The desire to make traditional communication media accessible for all people has resulted in the development of different assistive technologies from early innovations such as braille for print (1829) to assist people with vision impairment to read and write, captioning for film (1949), television (1972), and home videos (1980) for people hard of hearing, audio description for film and television (1988) for people with difficulties seeing, and the more recent live captioning for radio (2013) for people hard of hearing (Jaclyn Packer, 2015).[6]

The interest in enabling all people to use computer systems successfully and the development of assistive technologies to do so have a long history that goes back to the beginnings of computer development and the research conducted into speech synthesis at Bell Labs in the 1950s–1960s. Voice synthesis was an early goal: the IBM 7094, "A machine that talks and sings," was demonstrated in May 1961 to the Acoustical Society of America. This *vocoder* was a voice recorder synthesizer that responded to card-punch symbols. The capability of the voice synthesizer was brought to the attention of the general public in the 1968 film *2001: A Space Odyssey*, when Hal the computer sang the song Daisy.[7]

The first push for use of computer assistive technology by the general public in the US was for educational purposes. The 1970s, brought text-to-speech readers,[8] and the 1980s, when Apple was providing a free Apple IIe to every school in California, saw the introduction of the Adaptive FirmWare Card, an expansion card for Apple IIe that let users customize the keyboard for simple one or two key use (like switch gaming).[9] Features such as difficulty levels and use of image and/or audio to accompany text instruction, regularly included in children's educational and entertainment games, also became, by coincidence more than planning, accessibility features in gaming software. In hardware, it was often small developers, or gamers who had difficulty using hardware such as controllers, who adapted the technology. Larger gaming companies also began to address hardware needs of gamers with disabilities; in 1988, Nintendo offered a hands-free controller which could be operated by blowing or sipping through a straw (Wilds, 2020).

It wasn't until 1998, however, that there was a consistent push for mainstream gaming in the US to pay attention. The US federal government made funding for games used for educational purposes in classrooms dependent on the games being accessible. At the time, accessibility was not well defined for those developing games, so in 2003 the International Game Developers Association (IGDA)[10] created a Game Accessibility Special Interest Group (GASIG) which, in 2004, proposed 19 accessibility guidelines across impairment types that game designers could refer to. Based on only 20 games and limited in their applicability across all games, these first guidelines were revisited and given extensive updates in 2011 and 2015. IGDA's guidelines continue to be fine-tuned within the larger community of game developer organizations that are publishing best practices.[11] GASIG continues to support development of games for "gamers with disabilities of any sort" through round table discussions, and twice-yearly conferences, one in Europe, and one in the US. The conferences are noted for the window they provide into the process of development by gamers with disabilities. One pertinent observation in a presentation at the 2023 conference was that people can quickly lose capability through illness, or, in the case of the speaker, Jamie Knight, injury. Knight discusses "what can I do?" in context of autism and an injury that changed his life. Knight says that, ultimately, what he can do is framed by barriers society puts up. These are put in place by assumptions. If society changes its assumptions, barriers can be removed and Knight will be able to do more.[12]

With the development of the internet and the move to digital, traditional media (print, film, radio, television) became more readily available in one convenient online package. Features initially designed for desktop or laptop computers migrated to specialized technologies that were becoming part of the mainstream – smart phones, tablets, and e-readers used text-sizing, smart TVs used caption-sizing. Interested in bringing their technology to a larger market, communication companies such as Apple introduced features that improved accessibility as standard components of their smart phones and tablets.[13] These features increased use not only for those with different capabilities but also for a diverse market that included the young, the old, different language users, and those unfamiliar with technology. Entertainment companies, such as Sony who deliver game consoles and games, also claim a commitment to accessibility,[14] as do the companies who create games for them.[15] Whether driven by interest to increase markets or by public-spiritedness, better access is mandatory in an increasingly mobile world in which many services are now only available online.

Being able to play the game goes further than just accessing the game play. When asked, children speak up about the value of being able to play games and share what gaming accessibility really means to them, such as being able to join in and experience things the way other people do (a goal set by WHO for inclusion). Seth, who has a life-long progressive condition and uses a wheelchair, said when BBC interviewed him at age 13, that because he can't always join in running around with friends, he loves gaming. Playing video games is important to him "because it just helps me experience things like other people" (BBC, 2022).[16]

Social media has made it possible for individuals to add their voice to the discussion about disability and accessibility on social news websites such as Reddit, on social networking sites such as Twitter, and on game review blogs such as Kotaku. It is in these forums that we hear directly from players with disability of how they are affected by access, and increasingly, by representation. Current discussions of representation by adult game players trend towards the value of self-affirmation in seeing oneself in the media. In a review of *Animal Crossing: New Horizons*, Mike Fahey, who passed away in

2022 from health complications, echoed a sentiment expressed by other gamers with disability of the importance of being able to participate in gaming in typically realistic, not superhuman ways, and as a result, of being able to see themselves represented in the game. He tells us in the review that he spends half his life in a wheelchair because he is paralyzed from the waist down and has been this way for two years: for him it's a simple fact of life. The wheelchair in *Animal Crossing* isn't "anything fancy" and his own wheelchair would "crush it like a monster truck" but the simple fact that he can participate in the game in a realistic wheelchair makes him "happy." Different from its use in many fantasy games, *Animal Crossing* brings the wheelchair into everyday life and lets Fahey do all the things a regular guy does and, importantly, feel included because he can do them. He says, "The *New Horizons* wheelchair means a lot to me. I imagine it means a lot to many people. It might not be as cool as the wheelchair B.J. rides in the opening of Wolfenstein: The New Colossus, but it's also much less stupid" (Fahey, 2020).[17]

Personal testimonials on social media increasingly bring authentic voices in numbers not previously possible to the discussion surrounding disability and influence the current social model of disability, pushing it towards the WHO goal for both access and representation. By bringing game developers together with people with disability, conferences such as GASIG and GDC (Game Developers Conference) speed up the change. Accessibility design strategist, Aderyn Thompson, gave what she noted was the first-ever talk on representation at GDC 2019. Thompson said "The feeling of seeing even a glimpse of who you are in a positive light is profound. … It's a nudge that you are not alone, and more importantly, that you are welcome." She goes on to say, "The lack of representation – or even worse, bad representation – can reinforce stigma" (Thompson, 2019).[18]

Representation

Discussions about disability and games are most often about accessibility, not about representation. This is the natural outcome of the fact that the first concerns when computers were introduced to general consumers in the 1970s were for accessibility. Since the early 2000s, serious thought has been given to accessibility in games by those who develop and write about games (Wilds, 2020; Zallio & Ohashi, 2022). Representation of disability, which is different from accessibility, has had only modest attention. In the last decade, representation of disability has been increasingly written about by researchers (Cainelli, 2022; Ellis, 2011; Ledder, 2020; Shell, 2021). It is also receiving more attention in gaming media reviews and studies: a 2017 review of disability representation in games showed authentic representation was slowly increasing (Greenbaum, 2017); a 2020 article discusses the bad and the good representations in the most popular games (Parlock, 2020); Currys PC World study on Diversity in Gaming (2019) reports that in the games they reviewed,

54% showed physical disability with the remainder either mental, sensory, mental/physical, or sensory/physical disability (Currys PC World, 2019). Representation of disability in video games is distinct in its difference from accessibility. Accessibility provides for access for all players, whether the game shows a representation of disability or not. Representation is a narrative that creates meaning and adds to the perception the player has of a disability. It has different implications for people with disabilities and for people without disabilities. For a player, if there is a representation of their disability, it does not usually provide any new factual information about their disability, it may, however, influence self-perception. For players who do not have a disability, the representation may be their only contact with the disability and can provide information of the disability portrayed. It can begin to build a perception of disability, or it can reinforce an existing perception of disability. If these are inaccurate, there are implications for our current social model of disability. As noted by Thompson earlier, bad representation can reinforce stigma (Thompson, 2019).

The earliest representations of disability in children's games include Quasimodo, with curvature of the spine, in *HunchBack* (1983) and Captain Hook, with a prosthetic hook, in *Peter Pan, the Adventure Game* (1984).[19] *Hunch-Back* is a sidescroller with simple graphics, *Peter Pan* is a text adventure with some graphic screens. These both rely on familiarity with the story for the player's recognition of the disability. A full range of disabilities (Fahey, 2020) is not represented in games; mobility is the most often represented disability and the wheelchair is a recognizable symbol that predominates (Media Smarts, 2022).[20] The first children's games with realistic stories that portrayed a character with a disability were introduced in the late 1990s and the wheelchair featured in all of these games. The switch accessible *Camp Frog Hollow* (1996) showed a camper in a wheelchair, the first *Backyard Baseball Junior* (1997) introduced Kenny Kawaguchi, a baseball player in a wheelchair, and *Geoffrey Goes to the Fair* (1998) brought us Lennie the Lion, who uses a wheelchair. The quality of representation varied with the type of game and the commitment of the developers to representing disability thoughtfully (discussed later).

The best kind of representation, the kind that benefits both the social model and the players, should provide exposure and engagement that avoids stereotyping, distinguishes and adds understanding of the disability portrayed, and constructs authentic meaning for the player. With the complexities of narrative, visuals, mechanics, and game play, games differ significantly in how they represent disability because of genre, interest and experience of the development team, and the purpose behind adding the disability. This latter can range from an interest in expanding market reach, to an interest in inclusion based on stereotypical views of disability, to an interest that is backed by a greater depth of understanding of disability issues. The wheelchair proved convenient in all cases as a "person in a wheelchair offers no real identification challenges and can be seen to be disabled while still fitting in" (Media Smarts, 2022).

In looking at different representations across children's game, three main ways in which games deal with disability were identified. The early side-scrolling games in the 1980s, with simple pixilated graphics and jump movements, were only capable of cosmetic representation. Cosmetic representation provides a visual that has no reference to function or use and has no game play utility. The cooking simulation game *Overcooked* (2016) and language game *Peg and Pog* (2018) include characters with wheelchairs. The wheelchairs do not move. The characters do not function differently from other characters because they are in a wheelchair. There are no clues to its actual purpose, that is, a player would have had to learn from elsewhere that it is a mobility aid.

Representation can be incidental to the game narrative and used as the purpose for a storyline. Bentley in *Sly 2: Band of Thieves* is in a fight which leaves his legs damaged. In the following *Sly 3: Honor Among Thieves*, he is in a wheelchair which he must modify to be more effective in his role as Sly Cooper's sidekick. Together Sly and Bentley must convince their colleague Murray to return to their gang. He has left because he believes it was his fault Bentley was injured. The injury is a catalyst for a number of storylines, as is how Bentley adopts the wheelchair for his use.

Representation can be authentic. Authenticity can range from showing a character using their chair accurately as in *Geoffrey Goes to the Fair* (1998), to showing how a character came to be disabled and showing the difficulties of adjusting to life in a wheelchair, as in the game *Last Day of June* (2017). This game is about Carl, who was in an accident with his wife. She loses her life; he loses use of his legs. While there are many nuances and tangents for each of these approaches, as well as overlaps between them, at their simplest, these categories provided a practical way forward for our enquiry.

Why Study Representation in Video Games Rather than Other Media Such as Television?

The simple answer is twofold: because of the growing ubiquity of games and because repetitive interactivity sets schemas and synapses solidly at a young age.

Video games designed for children had their beginnings in the psychologist Seymour Papert's interest in using computers as a learning environment in the 1960s. Papert had studied with Jean Piaget in Geneva and brought his interest in constructivist learning and child development to MIT in the 1960s. With his team, he created game-like learning with programmes such as *LOGO* that could be used by children as young as three. In the 1980s parents' belief that educational games were better than entertainment games, especially for their younger children, gave way as edutainment games, which appealed to both parents' interest in education and children's inherent interest in play, became a mainstay (Madej, 2018). Since then, video games have increasingly become a greater part of children's daily engagement with media for both entertainment and education.

Statistical data on use is difficult to compare as each organization has its unique requirements and survey questions do not correlate. Ages for the term "children" range and include 10–16, and up to 18. That being said, in the US, *The Common Sense Census on Media Use by Kids Zero to Eight for 2020* shows that, on average, children 5–8 play games for 40 minutes daily, children 2–4 play for 15 minutes. Parents report 12% of children under 2 have used mobile media to play games.[21] For children 8–12, the 2019 Census for children aged 8–12 shows 46% play games daily.[22] In the UK, Statista shows that in 2021, 25% of children 3–4, 41% of children 5–7, and 72% of children 8–11 (ever) played video games online.[23] A 2019 report by the Children's Commissioner in the UK states 93% of children between 10 and 16 play video games.[24]

The addition to their lives of smart phones and tablets, which now incorporate traditional media through online availability, makes it difficult to know precisely what media children are using. They may, for instance, be watching a film or TV series, playing a game, or engaging in social media to talk with a friend, when they are using a smart phone. For parents, games can be safe bets for educational, fun content for children of any age. Parents who provide children under 2 access to media say they do so for education (70%), fun (52%), or so they can get some work done (52%). In past years, any parent who has had a group of children in the back seat of a car or van on a road trip, or even just transported them from point A to point B, was tempted to include handheld games as a detraction; today, providing a tablet or passing on own their smart phone is often the answer for a moment's respite. All these moments with media increase opportunities for exposure to representation. The games in the media mix provide a way for children to interact with the characters who have disabilities and to repeat that interaction often.

While serious social topics such as bullying have been looked at for two decades in media online environments (Antle, 2004; Antle, 2019; Ventä-Olkkonen, 2021) and in games (Madej, 2017), the topic of representation of disability has been better addressed for other media such as television. A recent analysis of 50 television programmes for young children shows a lack of representation and notes that what exists is often token, didactic, stereotypical, or worse, a misrepresentation with characters with disabilities represented as villains (Hopster, 2019; Smedley, 2015).[25]

Since the first apps for children were developed by Papert and his team at MIT in the 1960s, the majority of research into children's cognition and games has focused on the development of skills such as math, science, and language skills. More recently, research has focused on the social and emotional relationship with video game characters that encourages skill development. Educational games have used the premise of a familiar friend encouraging learning since the 1980s. In *Clifford's Fun With Letters* (1988), *Arthur's Math Adventures* (1999), and more currently *Dora's Number Pyramid Adventure Game* (2023), characters originally from books and television series continue to be recruited to increase learning. Recent studies have found that when the social and emotional relationship with such characters, now called a parasocial relationship, is used to encourage skill development, it has been found to increase learning because of the familiarity which exists from previous experiences (Blumberg, 2019). Such studies continue to focus on games as learning tools for skills, rather than as experiences that change perception.

The Chapters

One way we can better understand why we hold certain views as adults about disability is by knowing how our perceptions are formed. For this we need to go back to how our views were developed throughout our childhood. We can then apply this understanding to analysing games. The next section outlines information each chapter discusses. The first two chapters are on cognitive development, Chapter 2 on schema, play, dreamworlds, and cultural toolsets, and Chapter 3 on cognitive development and discusses both behavioural and neurobiological theories. Topics are illustrated with examples from PEGI 3 and PEGI 7 games. This is a base for a discussion of how the representation in different video games can be interpreted by children in Chapters 4 and 5. Chapter 4 discusses games which have characters with physical disabilities, Chapter 5 looks at games with characters with neurodevelopmental disabilities. Chapter 6 provides information on how games are age rated and provides context for the different rating systems which are used for children's games. Chapter 7 summarizes.

In More Detail

Chapter 2 begins the discussion of what happens cognitively when children are playing. First, schema is introduced as the framework of experience that humans construct from birth throughout their life and that helps them relate to and integrate information. The chapter goes on to explain how children learn through play as they invest all the "toys" around them, from a mote of dust to the sound of a voice, with meaning, theory based on psychologist Melanie Klein's early studies in the 1920s. The discussion on play continues with the explanation for why children don't "disbelieve" the way adults do. Children's experience of the real world is limited. They create a circle of play populated with their personal version of the world which is a negotiation of the external world and their own experience, a concept introduced into child development theory by W.D. Winnicott, and into game theory by Johann Huizinga. Shaping children's engagement with experiences are cultural toolsets that have, over generations, evolved into societal norms. As children grow older and engage more with an external world, the cultural norms set by their family are challenged by today's easy internet access to global media and others' viewpoints.

Chapter 3 looks at the twin underpinnings of our understanding of child development, behavioural psychology and neurobiology. Traditionally society has studied children's behaviour through observation. The chapter summarizes key theories developed since the 1930s about stages of human development and identifies distinct characteristics and recognizable milestones (Jean Piaget, Jerome Bruner, Lev Vygotsky) as well as Kieran Egan's study of imaginative understandings. Included is research from the educator Mark Fettes which explains how, through cultural tools they are provided, children develop their abilities for grasping concepts of substance, process, and integration for engaging with the world. The chapter considers children's ability to engage with games at different ages and shows how they might react to situations in which characters with disabilities find themselves. It discusses a child's cognitive ability to engage with the tasks which characters must undertake to succeed within the narrative and skill level of the age rating of a game, such as PEGI 3, PEGI 7, or ESRB Everyone. The chapter moves on to neuroscience. It introduces the development periods suggested by synaptic activity which support the establishment and then conservation of perception through the interaction and repetition provided by games. The chapter also presents research on mirror neurons, how these make real the aesthetics of images, and how this sense of reality might play out in integrating representations into a child's schema of disability.

The discussion of behavioural and neurobiological research provides the fundamentals of child development which can now be brought to bear to framing children's experience with games. Chapters 4 and 5 look at the representation of disability in individual games and map against them aspects of development identified in Chapters 2 and 3. Chapter 4 addresses games with characters with physical disabilities. While the games span a 40-year timeline beginning with *HunchBack* (1983), the analysis is presented in categories rather than in time sequence. It discusses games as cosmetic, incidental, and authentic and looks at the most common disability represented in games, mobility, first. It goes on to discuss games that feature characters with physical disabilities more difficult to represent and less often represented (possibly but not necessarily correlational) such as blindness and deafness. The chapter also addresses current use of virtual reality in the game *Moss* (2018).

Chapter 5 continues in the footsteps of Chapter 4 by mapping games that address difficult to represent neurodevelopmental disability against child development within the categories, cosmetic, incidental, and authentic. In this chapter as well, the discussion is not presented in time-line sequence. Following the discussion about the character Nemo in the previous chapter, this chapter first looks at Nemo's friend Dory, who has short-term memory loss, and then at other games for younger children with familiar characters such as Piglet from Winnie the Pooh, who displays classic signs of anxiety. It moves on to games for both younger and older children which show characters with neurodevelopmental disorders such as ADHD, autism, and dementia and which hope to bring a sense of realism to disabilities that are emotionally challenging to live with and that may be disturbing to encounter in gameplay. Chapter 6 explains the EU PEGI and US ESRB rating systems that categorize games for their suitability for different age groups. It describes the needs that brought about the creation of these rating groups and the differences between them. It shows how limited ESRB is for guidance and why advocacy groups in the US such as Common Sense Media have set up independent rating systems. Rating systems in other jurisdictions around the world are also mentioned. In addition, there is a discussion of how games with these rating systems map against cognitive development.

Chapter 7 returns to Lennie and *Geoffrey Goes to the Fair* and notes that representation of disability ranges in providing a meaningful experience that increases understanding. The chapter summarizes that some progress has been made in representing more types of disability, with increased authenticity and sensitivity to both the needs of those being represented and those playing the games. It concludes with comments from players with disabilities on how representation affects them when it is present in games they play.

Notes

1 This approach to movement was first used in 1987 by Amanda Goodenough in her innovative HyperCard interactive digital story, *Inigo Gets Out*. Playthrough: https://www.youtube.com/watch?v=MxN8ZlIAwsI, Archived game: https://archive.org/details/hypercard_inigo_gets_out

2 Information about the development of *Geoffrey Goes to the Fair* by Apptastic Software Inc. was acquired through a personal interview with Warren Pratte (Pratte, 2021). Playthrough of the game: https://www.youtube.com/watch?v=pXIJK1iNk_Q

3 The manuscript is available for download at https://www.academia.edu/82089486/_Fragile_Avatars_Representations_of_Disability_in_Video_Games.

4 Its scope is limited to North America and the UK (and with apologies, not all evenly).

5 Language used to describe differing capabilities is in flux. The best practice reference for this book is https://www.acedisability.org.au/information-for-providers/language-disability.php and https://adata.org/factsheet/ADANN-writing

6 https://hackaday.com/2021/04/14/history-of-closed-captions-the-analog-era/, Captioning Timeline Highlights, https://dcmp.org/learn/25

7 Hal sings Daisy, https://www.youtube.com/watch?v=E7WQ1tdxSqI. The original IBM 7094 speaking and singing, https://www.youtube.com/watch?v=IlBmbt8IVv4

8 1976, Kurtzweil Reading Machine for the Blind (Optical Character Recognition and Text to Speech).

9 Paul Schwejda and Judy McDonald describe the development of the Adaptive Firmware Card (AFC), https://www.youtube.com/watch?v=xu40fnC94Hk&t=10s. For more detail of set up and use possibilities, see https://gswv.apple2.org.za/a2zine/Docs/AdaptiveFirmwareCard.txt

10 https://igda.org: Established in 1994, the International Game Developers Association (IGDA) "is the world's largest nonprofit membership organization serving all individuals who create games." The association has over 100 chapters around the world.

11 A timeline of IGDA reports (with links) from 2004 to 2021 is available at https://www.gamedeveloper.com/audio/a-history-of-game-accessibility-guidelines.

Following this original report, the Norwegian Medialt organization published a set of 34 game accessibility guidelines, in 2012 CEAPAT published Best Practices in Video Games, a group of researchers and game designers, including the BBC published Game Accessibility Guidelines (GAG) and AbleGamers published Includification, 2012. In 2018, AbleGamers published Accessible Player Experience APX. Companies such as Microsoft publish their own guidelines. All guidelines seem to be updated regularly. More recently there have been guidelines suggested for VR games from both researchers and tech companies such as Oculus (Heilemann, Zimmermann, & Münster, 2021; Yuan, Folmer, & Harris, 2010).

12 GAConference 2023, https://www.youtube.com/playlist?list=PLVEo4bPIUOsk7rv gPy8bBLZBruIEM5Apa. Jamie Knight at GAConference 2023, https://www.youtube.com/watch?v=plDRQrX6RW4&list=PLVEo4bPIUOsk7rvgPy8bBLZBruIEM 5Apa&index=2

13 In 2022, 18 accessibility features including voiceover, magnifying screen, and switch control were available on the iPhone and iPad. https://www.imore.com/accessibility-iphone-ipad

14 https://caniplaythat.com/2021/07/07/sony-wants-its-studios-to-explore-new-innovative-ways-for-accessibility/

15 In an interview with the developer Naughty Dog, the Verge notes that *The Last of Us Part 2* has "Around 60 Different Accessibility Options" at https://caniplaythat.com/2020/06/01/the-last-of-us-part-2-accessibility-interview-the-verge/

16 "Children speak out about games Gaming: Video games 'help people with disabilities like me'" at https://www.bbc.com/news/uk-wales-63634982

17 "I'm So Happy There's a Wheelchair in Animal Crossing: New Horizon" at https://kotaku.com/i-m-so-happy-there-s-a-wheelchair-in-animal-crossing-n-1842492728

18 GDC Showcase: "You Can Take an Arrow to the Knee and Still Be an Adventurer" at https://www.youtube.com/watch?v=Vb39BFs1UK0&t=1s, Teal Sherer: "Video Game Representation" at https://newmobility.com/video-game-representation/

19 There is an image of Captain Hook with his prosthetic hand as the first screen in the game. There is little that is said about the Captain's hook in the dialogue. The game comes with a copy of the J.M. Barrie book. Reviews say that the game is not successfully played without reading the book. A later section discusses the video games which rely on earlier media for a fuller picture of the characters. Complete playthrough of the game at https://www.youtube.com/watch?v=XdRoQh1Qo3Q

20 Current data from Currys PC World analysis of characters with disabilities identifies Physical, Sensory, Mental, Physical/Mental, and Sensory/Physical as categories with 54% of characters with physical disabilities (Mental Health and Disabilities, 2018).

21 https://www.commonsensemedia.org/research/the-common-sense-census-media-use-by-kids-age-zero-to-eight-2020

22 https://www.commonsensemedia.org/research/the-common-sense-census-media-use-by-tweens-and-teens-2019

23 https://www.statista.com/statistics/274427/online-gaming-among-children-in-the-uk-by-age-group/

24 https://assets.childrenscommissioner.gov.uk/wpuploads/2019/10/CCO-Gaming-the-System-2019.pdf

25 https://www.theguardian.com/sustainable-business/2015/jul/28/childrens-tv-representation-disability-nickelodoen-disney-bbc

Works Cited

Antle, A. (2004). Supporting children's emotional expression and exploration in online environments. In *IDC '04 proceedings* (pp. 97–104). ACM Digital Library.

Antle, A. A. (2019). EmotoTent: Reducing school violence through embodied empathy games. In *Proceedings of the 18th ACM international conference on interaction design and children* (pp. 755–760). New York, NY: Association for Computing Machinery.

Bakhtin, M. (1982). *The dialogic imagination: Four essays* (M. Holquist, Ed., & C. E. Holquist, Trans.). Austin, TX: University of Texas Press.

BBC. (2022, November 23). *Gaming: Video games 'help people with disabilities like me'*. Retrieved from BBC News: https://www.bbc.com/news/uk-wales-63634982

Blanck, P. (2019). Why America is better off because of the Americans with Disabilities Act and the Individuals with Disabilities Education Act. *Touro Law Review, 35*(1), 605–618.

Cahill, S. E. (1995, Autumn). Reconsidering the stigma of physical disability: Wheelchair use and public kindness. *The Sociological Quarterly, 36*(4), 681–698.

Cainelli, E. A. (2022, December 24). Neurodevelopmental disorders. Past, present, and future. *Children (Basel), 10*(1), 31.

Currys PC World. (2019). *Mental health and disabilities* (C. P. World, Producer). Retrieved from Diversity in Gaming: https://techtalk.currys.co.uk/tv-gaming/gaming/diversity-in-gaming/games-and-disabilities.html

Egan, K. (1997). *The educated mind: How cognitive tools shape our understanding.* Chicago, IL: University of Chicago Press.

Ellis, K. A. (2011). *Disability and new media.* New York, NY: Taylor and Francis.

Fahey, M. (2020, March 25). *I'm so happy there's a wheelchair in Animal Crossing: New Horizons.* Retrieved from Kotaku: https://kotaku.com/i-m-so-happy-there-s-a-wheelchair-in-animal-crossing-n-1842492728

Goering, S. (2015, June). Rethinking disability: The social model of disability and chronic disease. *Current Reviews in Musculoskeletol Medicine, 8*(2), 134–138.

Greenbaum, A. (2017, February 14). *Disabilities in video games are more realistic than you think.* Retrieved from Gamespresso!: https://www.gamespresso.com/2017/02/disabilities-video-games-realistic-think/

Heilemann, F., Zimmermann, G., & Münster, P. (2021, October 20). Accessibility guidelines for VR games – A comparison and synthesis of a comprehensive set. *Frontiers in Virtual Reality, 20 October 2021 Sec. Technologies for VR, 2.* https://doi.org/10.3389/frvir.2021.697504.

Hopster. (2019). *Is TV making your child prejudiced? A report into pre-school programming.* Retrieved from https://hopster_wordpress_v2.storage.googleapis.com/Hopster-Predjudice-Report-DIGITAL.pdf

Jaclyn Packer, K. V. (2015, March-April). An overview of video description: History, benefits, and guidelines. *Journal of Visual Impairment & Blindness*, 83–93.

Ledder. (2020). On dis/ability within game studies. In R. Garland-Thomson & K. Ellis (Eds.), *Interdisciplinary approaches to disability looking towards the future* (Vol. 2). New York, NY: Routledge.

Madej, K. (2017). *Taking on serious topics in children's entertainment games.* Retrieved from Computers in Entertainment: https://cie.acm.org, Academia.

Madej, K. (2018, April). *Children's games, from Turtle to Squirtle* (N. Lee, Ed.). Retrieved from Encyclopedia of Computer Graphics and Games: https://link.springer.com/content/pdf/10.1007/978-3-319-08234-9_103-2.pdf

Media Smarts. (2022). Common portrayals of persons with disabilities. Retrieved from Media Smarts: https://mediasmarts.ca/diversity-media/persons-disabilities/common-portrayals-persons-disabilities

Mental Health and Disabilities. (2018). (C. P. World, Producer). Retrieved from Diversity in Gaming: https://techtalk.currys.co.uk/tv-gaming/gaming/diversity-in-gaming/games-and-disabilities.html

Oliver, M. (1996). *Understanding disability: From theory to practice*. New York, NY: St. Martin's Press.

Parlock, J. (2020, January 8). *Video games and disability: Looking back at a challenging decade*. Retrieved from Polygon: https://www.polygon.com/2020/1/8/21056713/disabilities-video-game-characters-inclusion-accessibility-decade-in-review

Pratte, W. (2021, August 17). *Geoffrey goes to the fair* (K. Madej, Interviewer).

Schweik, S. M. (2009). *The ugly laws: Disability in public*. New York, NY: NYU Press.

Shell, J. (2021, March 13). What do we see: An investigation into the representation of disability in video games. *arXiv:2103.17100*.

Smedley, T. (2015, July 11). *Children's TV pretends disability doesn't exist*. Retrieved from Guardian Sustainable Business: https://www.theguardian.com/sustainable-business/2015/jul/28/childrens-tv-representation-disability-nickelodoen-disney-bbc

Switzer, J. (2003). *Disabled rights: American disability policy and the fight for equality*. Washington, DC: Georgetown University Press.

Thompson, C. (2019, March). *GDC Showcase: You can take an arrow to the knee and still be an adventurer*. Retrieved from YouTube: https://www.youtube.com/watch?v=Vb39BFs1UK0&t=1s

Ventä-Olkkonen, L. A.-J.-C. (2021). CHI against bullying: Taking stock of the past and envisioning the future. In *DIS '21: Designing interactive systems* (pp. 734–748).

Wilds, S. (2020, January). *For all the players: A history of accessibility in video games*. Retrieved from Gaming Bible: https://www.gamingbible.com/features/games-for-all-the-players-a-history-of-accessibility-in-video-games-20200124

Yuan, B., Folmer, E., & Harris Jr., F. C. (2010, June 25). Game accessibility: A survey. *Universal Access in the Information Society, 10*, 81–100.

Zallio, M., & Ohashi, T. (2022). The evolution of assistive technology: A literature review of technology developments and applications. In *Preprint of AHFE international conference, 2022*.

2 Child Development 1

Schema, Play, the Dreamworld, and Societal Norms

Building Schema

Since the early 1900s, our knowledge of how children learn has stemmed first from behavioural psychology, and then, with the development of EEGs in the 1930s, from neurobiology, direct study of the brain. Before we look at what we've learned from these two methods of study, it is useful to look at how humans internalize life experience and create meaning for themselves: how they develop their perceptions. Humans begin to construct a framework of knowledge and meaning from birth as they gather impressions through social interaction within their cultural environment. Experimental psychologist Fredric Bartlett, in his research into memory in the 1920s–1930s, theorized this framework as schema (Bartlett, 1932; Rumelhart, 1980; Wagoner, 2017).[1] Schema have been called mental models, but the term does not fully represent the dynamic and transactional nature of schema (Dewey & Bentley, 1949). Schema is better defined as an ongoing construction of short narratives that are added to and changed with each new experience (Engel, 1995; Schank, 1990). In laying down their scaffold of information, children find commonalities and differences that link what they are seeing to what they are doing and what happens when they do it; these associations become a part of the schema. Schemas overlap and intersect as they grow into a comprehensive and integrated system of information. The system is always in the background accumulating experiences and adding depth and breadth to a person's understanding. It is always there to refer to when a new experience needs to be interwoven and the entire system is drawn on when a new schema is constructed or an existing one added to (McVee, Dunsmore, & James, 2005). An existing schema can make a new but related experience easier to integrate, but it can also bias the new schema because of previous associations (Pudhiyidath, 2020). With repetitive reinforcement, a schema based on stereotypical ideas and stances becomes more established because it has more supporting experiences, this is analogous to the durability of reinforced synaptic connections (Bruer, 2002). Introducing non-stereotypical combinations creates more flexible schemas and open-mindedness (Vasiljevic & Crisp, 2013). While new

DOI: 10.4324/9781003430445-2

experiences can add to and change an existing schema, the original experience is always there, part of the scaffolding.[2] Importantly, schemas cover varying levels of abstraction from objects to cultural values and incorporate all aspects of human experience: physical, cognitive, emotional, social, and imaginative. This makes them complex and examples of schema building discussed later in the chapter are necessarily simplified to provide at least a preliminary picture of what may be occurring.[3]

Children's early interactions build schemas that are the foundational rungs of their knowledge, understanding, and meaning-making and result in a perception of the world that is the basis of the perceptions they hold as adults. Humans, whether they are children or adults, are constantly, and often unremittingly, exposed to new situations to which they are required to adapt and which they need then to bring into equilibrium with existing schemas. The way humans adapt experiences to their schemas and make them a part of their perception is through the useful concepts of assimilation and accommodation (Piaget, *The Construction of Reality in the Child*, 1954). With any new experience children will try to make sense of what is happening based on what they know. Children have had fewer experiences than have adults and any of their individual schema is not as deep as an adult's. They may need to reference a broad range of schemas because, as of yet, the one most pertinent to the experience may be quite shallow. If, because a child hasn't had a similar experience to build on and there is no exact reference, they will branch out and build on whatever is the closest frame of reference, whether it is accurate from an adult perspective or not (Young, 2005). This flexibility is an important function of children's early cognitive development and advantageous in introducing non-stereotypical ideas. When introduced to a new object or situation, children will first assimilate the information, that is they will apply concepts/understandings they already have to the new experience; they shape the unfamiliar with the familiar. Future experiences may encourage a change in their idea of the object and necessitate accommodation and creation of a new schema, an activity that is more difficult than assimilation because it requires a change in the cognitive structure of the scaffold. Whether it is assimilated or accommodated, successful adaptation of the new information brings it into equilibrium with the child's understanding of their world (Bormanaki, 2017).[4]

Examples

To show how a schema, which adults consider will add positive exposure to disability, will not necessarily do so, we will look at a 2D game intended for children 3–5, *Peg and Pog* (2018).[5] This is a language learning game for mobile phone or tablet with original audio in five languages which at first does not appear to show any kind of disability. It is described by the publisher, Kenikeni, as an immersive adventure in which two main characters *Peg and Pog* (and their cat Cosmo) have eight different interactive adventures, both mundane (grocery shopping) and exotic (flying in a hot air balloon over an African plain). The graphics are cute, front-only view animations with minimal movement (arms, legs, feet, smiles, eyes); there is no realism only similitude. The game allows for independent play for young children: it is simple and intuitive, with objects that move at a finger touch. Sound to text is provided as a part of the vocabulary-building second level which links text with key objects and animals and is accessed by clicking a book symbol in the top corner of the screen.

Each adventure features *Peg and Pog* and different animals. The eighth adventure, a musical birthday party, is different from the others: *Peg and Pog* are part of a diverse group of friends: two boys, four girls – one person of colour, one of east Asian descent, one wearing glasses, and one (a girl) in a wheelchair. The game opens on a room with a table in the right front and a high stage at the back. Objects begin to appear in the center of the stage, and then slide forward to the floor in front of the stage. These objects can then be moved to an appropriate place with the touch of a finger: a guitar and a keyboard are moved to the stage, various glasses and cakes are moved to the table. Then a girl in a wheelchair appears mid-stage. Like the objects before her, she also floats forward to the floor. She waves her arms back and forth. A cake appears. She is the birthday girl. Clicking on her creates a small jump movement. Her friends, which include *Peg and Pog*, also appear. With a click, all of the friends can be made to jump in exactly the same way as does the birthday girl. Cosmo appears as a DJ on stage, and they all begin to dance. The girl in the wheelchair waves her arms and the five friends wave their arms as well. They also move their feet. The girl in the wheelchair does not move hers. There is a ramp on the left side of the stage. The player can move a friend along the floor to the ramp where they will glide up to the stage and be positioned to continue dancing. The friend can be brought back onto the floor the same way. Or the player can use their finger to float friends directly up onto the front of the stage. Again, all of the friends can be moved in the same way from the floor to the stage.

The simple graphics do not show how the wheelchair operates. The wheels do not move; the girl does not turn them with her hands. Our player, who is somewhere between 3 and 5 in this example, is not familiar with a wheelchair. How is the player to interpret this addition to the birthday girl? Where does this image fit into their existing schemas? Let us say that from previous media exposure, the player has a schema of a mermaid, who has a tail as an interesting addition to her body.[6] They might then think the birthday girl is similar to a mermaid and the wheelchair is part of her body, as is a mermaid's tail. This is assimilation: fitting the new into an existing schema – making for a girl-in-a-wheelchair-as-a-different-kind-of-mermaid.

Because schemas are dynamic, each new play of the game will reify the schema modified through this first assimilation. The second level of the game, the vocabulary, is a simple pairing of image with text. The chair is shown as an object which is separate from the birthday girl, although no explanation is provided of its purpose. Alternatively then, the schema can evolve to be: a normally abled birthday girl using some type of cool chair with wheels called a wheelchair. The learning options available to a child when playing the game on their own are now exhausted. Any additional change in their schema will have to come from some future experience that adds extra information: a discussion with an adult or more experienced sibling about the purpose of the wheelchair, seeing Tarah train for wheelchair sports in *Sesame Street*,[7] or Brian the Dog talk about disability in *Creature Discomforts* television ads,[8] or encountering someone in a wheelchair in the park. Any of these encounters will change the schema more extensively as these add to the understanding of the wheelchair's purpose. The more complex information will need to be accommodated, not only assimilated so that a new schema is created which is a better-informed version of the girl in a wheelchair – the wheelchair is a mobility aid for someone who has difficulty walking. Each additional experience of a person using a mobility aid will add complexity and depth to the new schema, bringing with it nuances of the wheelchair as an object, and of the personal and cultural values associated with its use.

This example uses as its player, a 3- to 5-year-old who does not have any familiarity with wheelchairs. If, however, the player was a child who was mobility challenged and was familiar with the purpose of the wheelchair through personal experience, then seeing their disability portrayed in a dynamic music scene by an animated and happy birthday girl who appeared on screen before the other dancers, even before *Peg and Pog*, and was front and center in the action, could be self-affirming – a positive implication. If the player knows of disability through a family member's use of a wheelchair, the same positive implication holds true. If their existing schema has negative associations with their disability or their family member's/friend's disability, then the music party will, in contrast, add a positive association to their schema (see nuancing the norm).

Our second example of building schema uses two games: *Geoffrey Goes to the Fair* from Chapter 1 and *Backyard Baseball Junior*. The following two game examples show how a schema that includes a wheelchair user is influenced by the way developers use language or image.

In Chapter 1 Lennie the Lion, one of Geoffrey's friends in the game *Geoffrey Goes to the Fair*, uses a wheelchair. The game was intended to be played by young children, many of whom, like those who played *Peg and Pog*, had not had any exposure to someone using a wheelchair. Through the depictions of Lennie as one of the gang who participated in all activities equally, Lennie added a schema of a wheelchair user as friendly, competent, and competitive.

Let us pretend that a few years later, children who played *Geoffrey Goes to the Fair* are playing *Backyard Baseball Junior*. In this hypothetical situation, children have had little or no other exposure to wheelchair use beyond Lennie the Lion. One of the player choices is Kenny Kawaguchi, a young athlete who, because of a mobility disability in his legs, uses a wheelchair. At the beginning of the game, kids are chosen for each team. When Kenny's turn comes up, he comments "Don't let this wheelchair fool ya', I can play."

Although Lennie the Lion is in a wheelchair, his ability to be able to race his friends down the street and play arcade games is not questioned and is not a factor in being included as one of Geoffrey's friends. Kenny, in order to join the team, must persuade the coach that his use of a wheelchair does not hinder his competency in playing the game. Because of Kenny's comment, the wheelchair schema children constructed from *Geoffrey Goes to the Fair* needs to assimilate three new ideas: one, doubt about competency of an individual in a wheelchair, two, doubt that someone in a wheelchair can be part of a team, three, the need for someone in a wheelchair to defend their competency in light of the aid.

Kenny is chosen for the team and soon proves his competency (he's a stellar player). The schema of a wheelchair user playing great baseball is introduced to counter the initial negative reference which, nevertheless, remains in the schema. After playing *Backyard Baseball,* representation of a user in a wheelchair is nuanced: Geoffrey's use of a wheelchair is a positive image of competency, Kenny's use of a wheelchair, because it must be defended as not being a liability, adds to the schema hesitancy about competency. If future experiences of people or characters who use wheelchairs (stories, images, parental support) are positive, then a positive attitude will be reinforced. If children go on to experience cultural attitudes, stories, and images that discriminate, vilify, or disparage, the negative schema will be reinforced.

Play: Children Learn from Their Own Perspective

In an earlier chapter we learned that computer games for children have been used to educate since Seymour Papert developed the LOGO program with his research team at MIT in the 1960s and used it in kindergartens with children aged 3–5. By the early 1970s, curriculum-based learning games targeted at ages ranging from 3 to 18 were being introduced into classrooms by innovative school systems such as MECC, the Minnesota Educational Computing Consortium. At the same time, the first entertainment home console system *Odyssey Home Entertainment System* became available to families. The 1980s brought commercial success to such edutainment games as *Reader Rabbit* (1983). By the mid-2000s, 40 years after Papert suggested games were an excellent tool to encourage cognitive development, game developers began to target parents of children as young as 6 months old. A computer game such as *Giggles Computer Funtime for Babies* (2006), suggested for 6–36 months, bases its simplest activities on a baby's interest in interacting physically with their environment, delight in seeing or hearing a result, and self-motivation to go on to the next experience. Such games are developed in anticipation that children will learn what is intended for them to learn by adults (not always the case) and will be entertained while doing so (almost always the case).

When child psychologist Melanie Klein began her study of children with affective disorders in the 1920s, she was interested in understanding their cognitive process. Through observation of patients as young as two, Klein found that children internalized their experience of the world outside of them through play. The act of play provided children with the interaction and control of objects necessary to integrate knowledge and understanding of those objects. For many adults, the word toy confers a low status to an object. Klein theorized that for a child, every object they come in contact with, whether a ball, a spoon, a book, or a word on a page, is a toy, to be played with, explored, and included in their increasing knowledge of the world around them. So too, is every person they meet. (Consider yourself a toy to a young child.) As they investigate an object, children view it from their own perspective, negotiate their own relationship with it, and invest it with their own images and emotions: they confer meaning on it (Kidd, 2004; Young, 2005). A ball, for instance, can introduce three-dimensional roundness; it can be pushed and made to move, to bounce, possibly to squish, to roll out of reach, and when, surprisingly, it hits one on the head when thrown by a sibling, hurt. When they first experience a ball, babies and toddlers do not internalize the meaning an adult confers on the ball. They work out what the object means to themselves, for themselves, within the context of their play. As they do not have the adult's experience to refer to, they can only understand the ball based on the schema they've constructed from their experiences of similar items up to that time. This is the same whether the object they encounter is a ball at age 6 months, or a video game avatar who uses a wheelchair, at age 4.

Klein's observations lead us to understand that children's game experience is their own, not what adults might want it to be. Parents might like to think the experience their children have of a game like *Peg and Pog,* which includes a person/avatar in a wheelchair, encourages understanding about the disability and even empathy with the person/avatar using the wheelchair. Unfortunately, without any narrative, mechanics, or game play purpose for the wheelchair, and without an existing schema that supports the adult's expectation, that understanding is unlikely to happen. More information is needed.

Characteristic of young children's play is making behaviours their own through repetition. Learning games like *Peg and Pog* take advantage of this characteristic by providing game play that encourages repetition of actions; the game doesn't tire, as a parent or sibling might. Repetition reifies the action and its associated values (Bower, 1976; Huizinga, 1949).[9] In *Peg and Pog* it adds solidity to the schema that a child is building for themselves of the musical party characters. The wheelchair has no noticeable effect as the birthday girl and the other dancers jump and move equally well at the behest of the player – over and over again until the actions are well ingrained (and as I'm doing in this discussion).

As a key factor in development, play provides the transitional place for young children to begin conceptualizing the meaning of an object separate from that object. Young children first only understand the material thing before them as an object. A wheelchair, for instance, is simply a chair with wheels. When a child sees a person who has difficulty using their legs, get into the chair, and manoeuvre it around, the wheelchair object begins to take on meaning for them. This happens over time with meaning eventually predominating over object. When objects begin to have meaning, play can become more imaginary (Tomasello, 2021; Vygotsky, 1978). Games like *Peg and Pog* do not have the mechanics or game play to help a child take the wheelchair from object to meaning on their own. Sandbox games are better at providing children an environment that encourages the type of pretend play in which meaning can develop further. The *Toca Life* series of games, which we will discuss later, is an example of a sandbox game that includes wheelchairs in its assets and provides opportunity for children to explore the meaning of a wheelchair through stories the children create, even though the wheelchair representation is cosmetic.

This chapter continues with why, for a child, a wheelchair can be considered a perfectly acceptable appendage to a human, as can a mermaid's tail, and not just an external aid.

Disbelief Isn't an Option

D.W. Winnicott worked with Klein in his early years as a clinical psychologist. Winnicott characterized the play experience for children as one in which they are intensely and completely preoccupied with an activity, a preoccupation that not only makes it difficult for them to admit any intrusion into the activity, it makes it equally difficult for them to leave the activity. This preoccupation creates a particular play space singular to the child that, while definable as outside the child, is yet not of the external world, rather it is a construct of the two: the space where their inner reality meets an outer reality. Children will always impose their own understanding of reality on any objects or experiences they bring into their play space. It is an "interplay of personal psychic reality and the experience of control of actual artifacts" (Winnicott, 1971, p. 47). This phenomenon, controlling actual artefacts within a play space of one's own making, is a strong characteristic of video game play.

Johan Huizinga, cultural historian, published his theories about Man the Player in the book *Homo Ludens, A Study of the Play Element in Culture* (1938).[10] He echoed both Winnicott's ideas about the primacy of play, and that in play humans create for themselves separate play spaces, "the arena, the card-table, the magic circle, the temple, the stage, the screen, the tennis court, the court of justice, etc., are all in form and function play-grounds, i.e. forbidden spots, isolated, hedged round, hallowed, within which special rules obtain. All are temporary worlds within the ordinary world, dedicated to the performance of an act apart" (Huizinga, 1949, p. 10).[11] His description of this world apart struck a chord with game theorists Eric Zimmerman and Katie Salen who reframed the enigmatic term Huizinga used, "the magic circle," as a requisite characteristic of video game play, "a special place in time and space created by a game" (Salen & Zimmerman, 2003, p. 95).

When children's preoccupation within their magic circle ends, they take the personal version of objects and experiences created within this "precarious world of shared realities, theirs, and what is objectively perceived" into the external world (Madej, 2014, p. 8). As young children have not yet acquired sufficient life references to bring to this world of shared realities an adult understanding of what is real or not real, while adults must suspend disbelief to envision a wheelchair as an actual part of our birthday girl in *Peg and Pog*, children simply do not disbelieve the idea.[12] Why? The educational philosopher, Kieran Egan, in his study of children's imaginative engagement with the world (see next section on cognitive toolsets) shows that when children are young, they learn to negotiate between binary opposites such as humans and animals. The options which are provided to them, such as mermaids and fauns, are no less real than are the humans in the stories they experience. These entities are not "pretend," but "real" constructs within their frame of reference. As a result of accumulating experience, by the time children are in grade 3, around age 9, they may have developed a more adult perception of commonly accepted realities, such as that Santa Clause, or Father Christmas, might not really exist. Games, however, because they continue to provide a magic circle which brings intense focus and engagement with stories players themselves create, continue to provide a sense of reality to "characters supernatural" (Coleridge, 1817).

Nuancing the Norm

The concept of schema shows that children's growing perception of the world around them is based on their experiences from birth. This experience is necessarily defined by the cultural group they are a part of and the society in which they live.[13] As children grow up, their culture provides them with strategies for dealing with the world around them. Strategies are the toolsets needed to manage daily life as well as deal with more abstract notions such as feelings, ideas, or purpose of life. Children's cognitive development is helped by the strategies or toolsets that are provided to them which have been centuries, if not millennia, in the making. Each generation expects their strategies will serve the next generation well, and unvarying use sets up a cultural norm of beliefs and expectations for children to continue the same way (Gauvain & Richert, 2022; Tomasello, 2021; Vygotsky, 1978). While norms are imparted to all children as part of daily life, no two children will reference their experience in exactly the same way.

A young child's world is very limited. Historically, young children were confined in their family circle with their view of the world consistently reinforced by immediate or extended family, and by the social circle surrounding the family unit. Viewpoints contradictory to the family's and the culture's norm were seldom introduced. The first media that could do so readily was print. With literacy rates in the UK in the 1870s at 70–75%,[14] and in the US at 20%[15] influence through print was still limited and, for young children, access was controlled by parents. With the emergence of films as a new information and entertainment source in the 1900s, no literacy was required for understanding and external influences more readily encroached on a family's sphere of influence. The introduction of media technology such as the telephone, radio, and television brought outside ideas directly into the home and the family unit.[16] Children were considered an audience even from the early days of these technologies with programming for them available on the telephone from 1911,[17] radio from 1922,[18] and on television from 1946.[19] Between 1953 and 1970, television replaced radio as the primary home entertainment medium (MacDonald, Marsden, & Geist, 1980). Children didn't, however, only listen and watch programming made specifically for them. Because of the nature of these broadcast media, they were exposed to whatever adults were listening to, and watching as well. In either case, the "latest" media exposed children to ideas from the outside world.

Fast forward 50 years. In our contemporary western world, by the time they are 3, many children have watched and played different types of media on their parent's smart phone or tablet. The iPhone came onstream in 2007. Market strategy aimed not only at business people or those who were tech savvy, but at as wide a market as possible. Accessibility features made it easier to use for those new to technology, for children and seniors, and for those with different capabilities.[20] The iPhone was quickly followed by the availability of iPhone apps via the App Store in 2008, and the iPad in 2010. Between 2010 and 2020, screen time use by children had shifted from television and game consoles to smart phones and tablets. In 2010 there were 60 million iPhone users; in 2020 there were a billion. In 2010, in the US, 3% of children under 8 owned smart phones, in 2020, 48% did (Rideout & Robb, 2020).

Smart phone and tablet technology with touch screen internet access is child friendly, and these two devices, together with the growth of social media, have made it simple for even young children to access many kinds of information from a wide range of online sources. Unsurprisingly, the Covid pandemic increased screen time (by 58%), particularly for school-aged children, as schooling went online.[21] The return to face-to-face learning may reduce screen time but the habit of learning and playing online, with access to resources that are not as culturally enclosed as they once might have been, is now even more entrenched than it was. So too is sharing and communicating ideas through social media, even for young children. *Toca Life* game, a game series from Sweden intended for young and middle-years children, has been downloaded "more than 849 million times in 215 countries."[22] The series has an online social media presence with children from many countries posting videos they have created (age restrictions on social media mean a parent has to set up the account for the child who wants to post).

The internet continues to introduce global influences to children through online games and nuances continue to be added to the schema of disability children have constructed within their cultural norms. Even with external influences adding new information to a schema, a child's place within their society will temper any shifts in viewpoint that the dynamic nature of schema allows for. As children get older however, and both their interest in autonomy, and their ability to achieve it, increases, cultural norms may fall by the wayside.

Notes

1 Although the idea of schema as organizing structure goes back to Emmanuel Kant in the 18th century, Bartlett's studies have been used extensively in studying cognition and child development from Piaget on and are more useful in mapping games against child cognitive development.

2 This has both benefits and detractions as social media, with its unerasable presence, has shown. Past peccadillos are always there in the background, ready to be brought forward to colour our impressions of, for instance, any new mention of a celebrity or politician. There is no way to escape the scaffold of information that has been built up.

3 Without this scaffold of information to build on, every experience would require continuous relearning a person's relation to people, places, objects, and events. Life, if possible at all, would be fraught with confusion and uncertainty, similar, but even more extreme, than that shown in the classic film Memento, in which the protagonist Leonard Shelby cannot form new memories because of short-term memory loss (he has anterograde amnesia) (Wicas, 2013).

4 Note that an adult's encounter with new information goes through the same process.

5 Example playthrough https://www.youtube.com/watch?v=w7CjHDlIc2g

6 *The Little Mermaid*, by Hans Christian Anderson, is a classic children's fairytale that has been adapted to numerous books, movies, and television programs.

7 Episode aired January 19, 1994, https://muppet.fandom.com/wiki/Episode_3178

8 https://www.theguardian.com/media/2007/nov/12/advertising.disability

9 The brain grows and develops through synapse formation; synaptic connections are reinforced by repetition (Bower, 1976; Bruer, 2002).

10 *Homo Ludens* was first translated into English for a Routledge edition in 1949. The revised translation, introduced in 1955, is the one most used.

11 The concept has been adapted by game theorists who use it to explain game phenomena (Salen & Zimmerman, 2003).

12 In *Biographia Literaria, Chapter XIV* Poet Samuel Taylor Coleridge suggested that readers would suspend disbelief of something implausible if provided sufficient "human interest and a semblance of truth" (Coleridge, 1817). The concept is also referred to in film and game studies.

13 Culture refers to the set of beliefs, practices, learned behaviour, and moral values that are passed on, from one generation to another in a group. Society means an interdependent group of people who live together in a particular region and are associated with one another. There can be different cultural groups within, for instance, European, UK, or North American society.

14 https://www.gale.com/binaries/content/assets/gale-us-en/primary-sources/intl-gps/intl-gps-essays/full-ghn-contextual-essays/ghn_essay_bln_lloyd3_website.pdf

15 https://nces.ed.gov/naal/lit_history.asp

16 In 1970, 96% of households in the US (https://americancentury.omeka.wlu.edu/items/show/136) and 93% of households in the UK (https://www.bbc.com/news/entertainment-arts-30392654#) had televisions.

17 In 1911, Howard Garis's *Three Little Trippertrots* featured as stories read nightly over the telephone at the N. J. Telephone Herald Company. https://earlyradiohistory.us/1912trp.htm

18 In 1922 in the US, *Uncle WIP*, Philadelphia WIP, https://www.broadcastpioneers.com/chrisgraham.html.

19 In 1946 in the UK, *For the Children*, https://www.bbc.com/historyofthebbc/anniversaries/june/for-the-children/

20 IOS features for iPhone and iPad included accessibility features for: "those with visual impairments, including blindness, color blindness, and low vision; and auditory impairments including deafness in one or both ears; physical or motor skill impairments, including limited coordination or range of motion; and learning challenges, including autism and dyslexia. It also includes features like Siri and FaceTime which can provide significant value for the blind or the deaf." https://www.imore.com/accessibility-iphone-ipad

21 JAMAPediatrics: Meta-analysis of 46 studies (29,017 children; 57% male; mean age, 9 years). (Madigan, Eirich, Pador, McArthur, & Neville, 2022).

22 https://play.google.com/store/apps/details?id=com.tocaboca.tocalifeworld&hl=en&gl=US#

Works Cited

Bartlett, F. C. (1932). *Remembering: An experimental and social study*. Cambridge, MA: Cambridge University Press.

Bormanaki, H. B. (2017, Sept). The role of equilibration in Piaget's theory of cognitive development and its implication for receptive skills: A theoretical study. *Journal of Language Teaching and Research, 8*(5).

Bower, T. G. (1976, November). Repetitive processes in child development. *Scientific American, 235*(5), pp. 38–47.

Bruer, J. T. (2002). *The myth of the first three years: A new understanding of early brain development and lifelong learning*. New York, NY: Free Press.

Coleridge, S. T. (1817). *Biographia Literaria, Chapter XIV*. Retrieved from Poetry Foundation: https://www.poetryfoundation.org/articles/69385/from-biographia-literaria-chapter-xiv

Dewey, J., & Bentley, A. (1949). *Knowing and the known*. Boston, MA: Beacon Press.

Engel, S. (1995). *The stories children tell*. New York, NY: Henry Holt and Co.

Gauvain, M., & Richert, R. (2022). *Cognitive Development*. Retrieved from Neuroscience and Biobehavioral Psychology: https://www.sciencedirect.com/science/article/abs/pii/B9780323914970000485

Huizinga, J. (1949). *Homo Ludens: A study of the play element in culture*. London: Kegan Paul Ltd.

Kidd, K. (2004). Psychoanalysis and Children's Literature: The case for complementarity. *The Lion and the Unicorn. 28.1 (2004): 109–30; 28*(a), 109–30.

MacDonald, J. F., Marsden, M. T., & Geist, C. D. (1980). Radio and television studies and American culture. *American Quarterly, 32*(3), 301–317.

Madej, K. (2014, November 13). Physical play in games: Children's engagement with narrative rhymes. Atlanta, GA: GVU Center Brown Bag Seminar Series.

Madigan, S., Eirich, R., Pador, P., McArthur, B., & Neville, R. (2022). Assessment of changes in child and adolescent screen time during the COVID-19 pandemic: A systematic review and meta-analysis. *JAMA Pediatrics, 176*(12), 1188–1198.

McVee, M. B., Dunsmore, K., & James, J. R. (2005, Wionter). Schema theory revisited. *Review of Educational Research, 75*(4), 531–566.

Piaget, J. (1954). *The construction of reality in the child.* New York, NY: Basic.

Pudhiyidath, A. H. (2020). Developmental differences in temporal schema acquisition impact reasoning decisions. *Cognitive Neuropsychology, 37*(1–2), 25–45.

Rideout, V., & Robb, M. B. (2020). *2020 The Common Sense Census: Media use by kids age zero to eight.* Retrieved from: https://www.commonsensemedia.org/sites/default/files/uploads/research/2020_zero_to_eight_census_final_web.pdf

Rumelhart, D. (1980). Schemata: The building blocks of cognition. In R. S. (eds), *Theoretical issues in Reading comprehension.* Hillsdale, NJ: Lawrence Erlbaum.

Salen, K., & Zimmerman, E. (2003). *Rules of play: Game design fundamentals.* Cambridge, MA: MIT Press.

Schank, R. C. (1990). *Tell me a story: Narrative and intelligence.* Evanston, IL: Northwestern University Press.

Tomasello, M. (2021). *Becoming human.* Cambridge, MA: Harvard University Press.

Vasiljevic, M., & Crisp, R. J. (2013, March). Tolerance by surprise: Evidence for a generalized reduction in prejudice and increased egalitarianism through novel category combination. *PLoS ONE, 8*(3).

Vygotsky, L. (1978). Mind in society: The development of higher psychological processes. Cambridge, MA: Harvard University Press.

Wagoner, B. (2017). Frederic Bartlett. In *Handbook of the philosophy of memory.* Routledge.

Winnicott, D. (1971). *Playing and reality.* London: Tavistock Publications.

Young, R. M. (2005, May 28). *MELANIE KLEIN I.* (I. P. Young, Producer) Retrieved Mar 15, 2016, from The Human Nature Review: http://human-nature.com/rmyoung/papers/pap127h.html

3   Child Development 2
Children's Cognitive Development

Behavioural Psychology and Neuroscience

Today, our understanding of cognitive development and how children integrate information and change it into knowledge is based in two types of study, behavioural, top down, and neurobiological, bottom up. Behavioural psychology looks at the visible manifestations of cognition, it makes deductions from watching children play. Neuroscience looks at the underlying mechanism that governs development, it examines children's brain directly. In his report on "The importance of play," Dr. David Whitebread explains that behavioural and neurobiological research shows "strong and consistent relationships between children's playfulness and their cognitive and emotional development" (Whitebread, 2012, p. 15).

Children's Cognitive Development – Behavioural Psychology

In the 1920s studies were conducted of very young children by psychologists Melanie Klein and D.W. Winnicott (discussed under play). This was followed by the work of three educational psychologists who became seminal and dominated child development research and theory in subsequent decades, Jean Piaget, Jerome Bruner, and Lev Vygotsky.[1] Their theories continue to shape our understanding of how children progress cognitively from birth to adulthood.

Characteristics identified by Piaget in his four stages of development that lend themselves to correlation to representation in games are also characteristics noted by Bruner and Vygotsky. Rather than providing a treatise on each theorist's work, the following presents characteristics that are immediately supported by game examples (Brunner, Vygotsky) or ones which are more easily correlated to games reviewed in the next section (Piaget). What does this mean? No games are referred to in the section on Piaget's theories. Games are used as examples for Bruner's theories, and in particular for Vygotsky's.

DOI: 10.4324/9781003430445-3

Jean Piaget, Four Stages

Piaget's observations led him to believe that children develop progressively through stages which, while they may vary in length, are age related and sequential, that children build mental representation by engaging with their environment, and that children develop their cognitive abilities through action, a process that became known as constructivism.[2] A proviso here is that Piaget's stages have been interpreted by many researchers and educators,[3] used scores of times in explaining development, been modified to include different characteristics, and have occasionally been discussed unfavourably. We use them here as a basic framework for discussion, acknowledging the complexity of the characteristics and the imprecision of at what age they may develop.

Each of the stages displays major characteristics and developmental changes. *From birth until age 18 months/2 years (sensorimotor)*, babies use all their senses to interact with their environment. *From 2 until age 6 or 7 (pre-operational)*, toddlers/young children learn to use language and represent objects with images and words. *From 7 until 11 or 12 (concrete operations)*, children learn to develop logical thought about physical processes. *From 12 until 16 (formal operations)*, children learn to think abstractly and consider hypothetical solutions when provided a complex problem. Each stage builds on the previous one, children need to be ready to move on, so that it would be difficult to progress if earlier stages weren't realized.

Piaget's second and third stages, pre-operational and concrete operations, correlate to PEGI 3 and PEGI 7 game rating ages. From approximately 18 months/2 years to 6 or 7 years of age, when, depending on their cultural environment, children are either at home under tutelage of their parents, or attending preschool, pre-kindergarten, kindergarten, and possibly their first year of elementary school, children start to become more aware of the space they occupy. They move from playing with objects to thinking about them in relation to the other things or activities surrounding playing with the object and so begin to build mental representation of their activities. To understand, they now ask how and why. This is the time when they begin to use language to express themselves, to communicate with others, and, also, to think. Language helps them structure their play. They speak to their toys, which have life and feelings and respond; they like to pretend play. They recognize and make symbols and progressively move to make their first letters. At this point, everything in their world relates to themselves. They are the centre of their world (self-centric) as they have not yet moved outside themselves to have a birds-eye view of either themselves or themselves in relation to others. Because of this, when playing with friends, their own view is still the right one, and although they provide sympathy with a kind arm and may acquiesce (with difficulty), collaboration is in its infancy, as judgements of a situation are based only on their own experience and are not necessarily logical (Donaldson, 1978; Piaget, 1972; Wood, 1998).

The concrete operations stage, from 7 to 11 or 12 years of age, builds on earlier development. Children begin to think logically about an object which they are manipulating physically and can construct that operation mentally without the object present. They progress to logical thought much more successfully if they can manipulate real objects (this is where constructivism stems from). Children begin to extend their self-centric view as they begin to see themselves as individuals within the world around them. This leads them to think about others, to wonder what they might think, how they might feel, and to engage in debate and collaboration more readily. They begin to question their world and their own place in that world, pushing the boundaries they've known and consider how others might think or feel about something (Piaget, 1972; Wood, 1998).

Bruner, Layered Modes, Cultural Context

Bruner also hypothesized that children moved through stages of development. He called these modes of representation, or ways knowledge is stored. He suggested that, unlike the progression of Piaget's stages, learning was a process of layering rather than superseding a previous mode. Learning was not necessarily tied to specific ages, that is, things can be learned at any age if taught appropriately to that age. Within a child development model, however, modes are tied to approximate age groups. *The Enactive mode, until 2* is the time when children's knowledge and thinking are object and action based. *The Iconic mode, from 2 to 6 or 7* is when children begin to represent things as images in their own minds and can maintain those images over time. *The Symbolic mode, 6 or 7* onward is when children are able to understand and learn through symbolic representation and to respond through symbol (music, math).

Layering rather than superseding is a useful construct when looking at games as it better explains how children of the same age bring different levels of ability to playing a game. Learning to play games is seldom a sequential step-by-step process. Modes with no hard and fast endings that can be accessed at any time imply that whether image is object and action based, or symbolic, children can access that mode of representation to learn to play the game.

Mentioned earlier were Piaget's precepts that children build mental representation by engaging with their environment and develop their cognitive abilities through action. Through their observation both Piaget and Bruner realized that children construct knowledge by actively engaging with their environment and that they are inherently motivated to do so. This led to the constructivist approach – learning by doing through contexts that make players motivated and able to learn and facilitate opportunities to go beyond the given – that led first to educational games but also underlies entertainment video games, as even for young children these are often self-directed (Wood, 1998). Games in which children can choose their own avatar, dress it, and then, for more successful play, collect attributes or power-ups, like the Hover

Pack (jet pack) Bentley in *Sly Cooper* can acquire, are "doing," they are actively engaging with a character who has a disability. But the ultimate self-directed constructivist activities are realized with sandbox games such as *Toca Life*, which lets children build whatever world they are inclined to in which children in wheelchairs can wheel around.

While Piaget focused on how logic as the capstone of cognitive development was achieved, Bruner emphasized communication, and the instruction provided in cultural environments through interaction with adults, as playing a key role in children's cognitive development. Adding cultural environment to the mix doesn't negate the characteristics Piaget identified, rather it brings in additional considerations especially when looking at the age things may happen. In a culture where children are encouraged and instructed by adults in certain activities early in their lives – reading, playing an instrument, dancing – they will become skilled in them at an earlier age than children do in other cultures. The same is true of concepts to which they are introduced, such as the value of diversity (Wood, 1998).

Vygotsky, Interpersonal Connections, Autonomy

But it was Vygotsky who underlined the importance of both culture and the interpersonal connections in a child's social milieu, insisting that it was only through interpersonal connections that children learned. Of course, a child's life *is* interpersonal connections. From the time they are born, they are taught what life is through careful guidance from adults that provides the order and cognitive toolsets necessary for development and enforces the societal norms mentioned in Chapter 2 (Vygotsky, 1985). As did Piaget and Bruner, Vygotsky observed children as going through developmental periods. He noted both children's dependence on social interaction and their move from total dependence on adults and towards autonomous thought and action as characteristics during their stages of development. Children's interest in gaining autonomy over their environment is inherent and consistent from infancy through older childhood at all age levels (Blunden, 2011).

From birth to 12 months (Infants)

- *Move from their total dependence on adults*
- Begin to learn tools like gestures and sounds for language
- Begin to learn to engage with environment to make things happen: i.e. pushing to make things move

From age 1 to 3 (Early childhood)

- *Develop self-consciousness as they initiate independent action in opposition to adults*
- Speech is a catalyst to this age

- Relate words to objects
- Learn to make basic social connections

From age 3 to 7 (Middle childhood)

- *Bring activities under own dominion and gain control of own behaviour*
- Experience world outside their home
- Learn to separate self from action and begin to generalize and reflect on own behaviour
- Begin to learn to act strategically as a way to find their place within their society and develop social skills required to do so

Between 7 and 13 (Older childhood)

- *Become further independent from parents*
- Develop faculty to reason and argue their position
- Role-playing games give way to rule-based games
- Begin to think abstractly

During early ages, the move to independent thinking is intrinsic, children need to develop independence to grow cognitively (and physically); in middle and older childhood stages, children move to a conscious interest in independent action, they not only need independence to grow, they want independence. Middle and older childhood coincides with increased exposure to outside influences and, often, a protect-and-preserve response from the family circle. As shown in *Nuancing the Norm* in the previous chapter, as children engage with media independently from influence of parents and society, the content they encounter in video games is often based on social practices different from those in their own society. When children see, and more importantly play, characters reacting differently to situations from the way they themselves have been encouraged to respond, they are given constructive experiences that encourage independent thinking. Today media is creating this situation earlier in their development. Their desire to be independent creates a context for including perspectives different from the norm in how they think.

   An earlier example of adding to schema can also be used here. Stigma may exist about disability in a culture. A child plays the game *Backyard Baseball Junior*, rated ages 5–10, in which Kenny Kawaguchi, who uses a wheelchair, introduces himself with a comment that acknowledges the social norm – the view that his disability is a liability, "Don't let this chair fool ya', I can play." The player sees the wheelchair as a liability, but when he looks at Kenny's ranking, he sees Kenny has many home runs, decides to take a chance, and picks him as a player for his team. Kenny goes on to hit home runs and becomes a major asset to the player's team. The child has independently taken a position different from the norm. They have made up their own mind to choose Kenny and have been rewarded for doing so. There is potential to then form an opinion different from the norm – that disability is not a liability, if only because it is to their advantage to do so (success is always a good motivator for change). As children strive to become autonomous and develop their own views, they may come to conclusions about disability that help counter the socially acceptable attitudes of concealing, shunning, or bullying that have been norms within their culture to which they have been exposed.

Vygotsky, Critical Periods and Mastery, Autonomy

There is always a gap created by newly developing needs when children must move from knowing how to do something to acquiring the next skill. Sometimes this gap is a precipice, sometimes only a low gully that must be traversed. In his theory of critical periods of stability and crisis, Vygotsky addresses this gap by explaining how children move from one stage of development to another as they pursue what they need to know and gain mastery of it. Critical periods are major times of transition (the precipices) and happen at ages 1, 2, 7, 13, and 17. They go something like this. Children enjoy the mastery of having learned something new (use their fingers to pick up cheerios, ride a tricycle, play chopsticks on the piano); this is the period of stability. Their new skills broaden their activity base and expose them to new and tantalizing opportunities (use a spoon, ride a bicycle, play *Claire de Lune* on the piano). They soon find that what they have learned will only take them so far in their exploration. They try, but they don't know how to do that something new, and so are unsuccessful. They try again, and again. Frustration grows; this is a period of crisis or critical period of instability that can be accompanied by tantrums, truculence, quarrelsomeness, and even aggression. As children continue to practise new skills, they achieve mastery, and a new stable period begins.

Different children take different paths through the frustration, some paths are more successfully negotiated than others. There are two factors that influence successful negotiation. One is sociocultural support. Children may have supportive siblings or adults who will help them get through the frustration by offering encouragement or providing advice. Or they may have internalized a cultural expectation, and supported by past teaching and a sturdy toolset that acts as guide, they can manoeuvre their way successfully through frustration (Bodrova & Leong, 2015). The other factor is their age, their behaviour (the average way they react to events), and their personal capacity (not skill, but higher order ability). Because societies have different expectations of the age at which their children develop certain abilities, the age of critical periods may differ, but their fundamental character remains the same (Blunden, 2008; Vygotsky, 1978).

We can see that the critical periods of stability/crisis will describe the process children go through during the major changes in their childhood. But the stability/crisis process, as a more shallow gully, is also a constant for all activities that require learning new skills (whether physical, social, or emotional) and continues beyond childhood through adolescence and into adulthood. It is easily observable in any activity that is skill based and requires players to have achieved certain skills to progress, such as playing piano, or in the case of this research, playing video games. It is perhaps more pronounced in playing games which are action/speed oriented and are designed to have players progress through levels of increasing complexity within the span of the game, which, for players new to the game, may require improving skills quickly to complete the game. Mastery is what moves players forward in games, whether arcade style games (*Buster Baxter*), simulation games (*Overcooked!*), or stealth games (*Sly Cooper*). Progression requires learning a character's moves and improving reaction time to match speeds necessary to complete tasks. Games don't let you "skip" to the next level. If a player is new to the mechanics of the game, they may need new skills to get to the end. They know this. To gain skill, actions are repeated over and over. But even though they know they need the practice, they may feel the repetition is not getting them anywhere. Play without rewards is frustrating, and players, especially younger players, get flustered and upset. This is the critical period. Repetitive practice eventually achieves the necessary skills, and mastery is gained. Eventually mastery is achieved for all levels in the game and the player moves on. Children tend to like to play above themselves and enjoy taking on games which challenge them and so learn to traverse gullies more quickly (Bodrova & Leong). As is the case with life skills, once learned, the skills can be used in future games of a similar nature.

Narrative games for children that represent disability in a more realistic and authentic manner (rather than frantic gameplay) still require a player to learn skills for manoeuvring through the game. In a narrative simulation game like *Beyond Eyes*, once the player learns the mechanics of the game, the skill level required remains constant until the goal is achieved. The task is to guide the blind Rae on a path so she can be reunited with her cat Nani. The player needs to learn to move like Ray by echolocation. There may be some frustration as unfamiliar game mechanics are learned, but the stability/crisis period is different, it does not have the same pressure as it would with a game which is speed-based, such as *Overcooked!* Rather than continuously ramping up skill levels to keep up with increased speed or complexity of action, the story encourages involvement with the character's needs. Mastery begins to include awareness and understanding of the character and not only learning to make them move faster. This is also the case in the representation of the cognitive disability dementia, in *Ether One*. Jean Thompson must learn to deal with the confusion caused by her deteriorating cognitive abilities in order to move through the game successfully. Here the anxiety the player may feel in the period of crisis before gaining mastery is intended to be ever-present as it echoes the anxiety of the character.

The practice and repetition at the heart of gaining mastery sets schema and establishes synapses, the physical connections our brain makes, more permanently; any associated perceptions being created of a disability can become fixed and more difficult to change in later years.

Egan, Language Strategies, Toolsets

In his recognition of culture and interpersonal relationships as foundational to children's development, Vygotsky identified that strategies which make up cognitive toolsets are specific to each culture. The educational philosopher Kieran Egan takes these cognitive toolsets and notes that we use language to mediate between ourselves and our environment and take our norms forward through narratives.[4] Egan suggested that cognition is a collaborative venture between rationality and imagination, that quality of thinking which enables humans to look beyond and ask "what if." In common with other theories that identify children's development as going through stages, Egan identified five different ecological zones of understanding children go through from birth through later teen years – somatic, mythic, romantic, philosophic, and ironic. They are considered ecological because they are based on local and natural language strategies with corresponding toolsets that have evolved to help mediate learning and development during each age period. Of interest to our purpose of discussing PEGI 3 and PEGI 7 games are mythic and romantic understandings, mythic during which children are introduced to oral and written language (approximate ages 3–7), and romantic, during which children become more aware of self, the outside world, and want to learn how they fit into that world (approximate ages 8–14) (Egan, 1997). Similar to Bruner's modes, zones of understanding layer rather than supplant each other, and tools are accumulated rather than superseded. Following are examples:

Mythic Understanding Tools, ages 3–7:

- *Binary Structuring* helps children negotiate between two opposites such as
  - good/bad
  - give/take
  - active/passive
  - black/white
- *Binary Structuring* helps children experience the "in between" of opposites
  - give/take – share
  - good/bad – mischievous
  - active/passive – anticipating
  - black/white – grey
- *Binary Structuring* helps children to mediate other binary opposites
  - life/death – ghosts
  - nature/culture – talking plants and animals
  - humans/animals – mermaids and sasquatches

- *Metaphor* adds to depth of understanding
- *Rhyme and Rhythm* engage children physically and aesthetically and help them remember stories
- *Games and Drama* offer different ways to explore stories and express ideas
- *Jokes and Humour* let children explore how language affects others
- *Mystery and Puzzles* suggest interesting facts are waiting to be discovered

Romantic Understanding Tools, ages 8–14:[5]
The move to questioning the world, exploring it, and wondering what it might be like to be somewhere, or something is assisted by

- *A Sense of Wonder*
- *Association with Heroes*
- *Exploring Extremes*
- *Testing Limits of Experience and Reality*
- *Collecting and Creating Sets*
- *A Sense of the Ideal*
- *Revolt and Idealism: Interest in human hopes, and passions*

While certain language tools are introduced and predominate during a zone of understanding, once learned, they are part of children's inventory of ways to investigate anything whatsoever they are curious about at any time. *Jokes and Humour*, for instance, while they may give way to *Associating with Heroes*, are not forgotten or forsaken. Along with epic battles and darker moments, *LEGO Star Wars: The Skywalker Saga* (PEGI 7) includes "slapstick antics, sight gags, and humorous dialogue."

In the discussion on suspension of disbelief (Chapter 2), we saw that for a young child a mermaid with a tail is real. This reality is a result of negotiating binary structures within their logic system. Such negotiation happens within their circle of play in which their reality and external reality meet and leads to thinking that humans can have a wheelchair as an intrinsic part of themselves.

Binary negotiation also leads to young children's belief that all anthropomorphic characters are real. Geoffrey, Lennie, and their friends in *Geoffrey Goes to the Fair* are real friends. After playing the game, if a child is unfamiliar with wheelchairs previously, then sees an actual person in a wheelchair, they don't say to themselves, "oh, that lion Lennie was just a fake and this is the real thing." The relationships young children build for themselves with their television and game friends are no less real than their relationship with their peers. The binary structuring from which this negotiation follows takes on more complexity and changes with age and experience from the reality it is for younger children, to the interest in fantasy it evolves into for older children, teens, and adults.

Fettes, Foundational Capacities

Cognitive tools, while different for each culture, share common foundational capacities or ways that humans grasp the different forms of order which they experience in the world. As children develop, they need to impose order on their vast new environment and identify the stable and recurring aspects of it. Foundational capacities can be seen as the way children reach out and "grasp" the hidden forms of order in the world. Using the grasping metaphor, tools in the five understandings are categorized into eight imaginative capacities. Three might be thought of as grasping the substantive, stable nature of the world, its "thingness," three as grasping its emergent, shifting nature, its "becomingness," and two as spanning the divide. The constant across understandings – grasping ideas (Fettes, 2010).

Tools of Substance

- Grasping regularity: the ability to perceive new forms of order in the world, and indeed to impose them on a sometimes, unruly reality
- Grasping detail: holding in one's imagination the individual richness of particular cases, situations, events, that makes them unique
- Grasping composition: developing a sense of the invisible relationships that bind such details together into a greater whole

Tools of Process

- Grasping possibility: developing an understanding of how such wholes may vary and change
- Grasping struggle: gaining a sense of what drives and what hinders change, and how this plays itself out in myriad variations
- Grasping indices or limits that help identify and characterize the possible limits of variation, change, and struggle

Tools of Integration

- Grasping wholes themselves, apprehending them as coherent entities with an identity sustained through time and space
- Grasping inconsistency: an appreciation for the ways in which the world does not always act as we imagine it will

How do these apply to playing games? As an example, the foundational capacity to grasp order (Tools of Substance) allows young children to find the order in games. From their first introduction to a game like *Peg and Pog*, they learn that to play the game they must use their finger and click on an image for anything to happen, then they must put their finger on top of a character to move it around. These are general rules they grasp which they can later apply to similar games. In *Peg and Pog*, they will find that if they click on some of the objects, a voice tells them what it is. If they click on an image with a book, the object will open in another screen and the audio is augmented by text. They learn to move through the game using specific actions, this is grasping detail. They compose in their mind an image of the rules and the details for a complete picture of what this genre consists of. They have grasped the whole. When children float the birthday girl to the stage the same way they float her friends, or slide them all up the ramp the same way, or use a click for the same action for all of them, they grasped as a whole that the girl and her friends have equal mobility.

Once children learn the foundational capacities, these become part of their thinking process. In games, their capacity to grasp order, detail, and composition means they can grasp the "form of order" in that world, so they can impose that order on the environment as they proceed through the game. If they did not grasp that regularity existed, they would need to relearn moves continually.

Cognitive Development – Developmental Neuroscience

> *Development is the process of life. Just as biology cannot be understood except in the light of evolution, psychology cannot be understood except in the light of brain development.*
>
> Cognition and Neural Development, Dan Tucker and Phan Luu (Tucker, 2012).

Age of Exuberant Activity

Neurobiological research examines children's brain directly. It looks at the underlying mechanism that governs development and furthers our understanding of age-related cognitive needs to provide a more complete picture of child development which can advance best practices in areas as diverse as planning education and health policy and designing toys and games.

The brain develops by making connections, these connections are called synapses and they can be mapped. The two main ways the brain is studied today are by EEG and MRI. The development of the Electromagnetic Encephalogram (EEG) in the 1920s advanced neurophysiologist's ability to experiment with recording patterns of electrical activity created by the synaptic activity of brain cells. Practically, the EEG measures such activity using electrodes placed on a person's scalp; electrodes can be either non-invasive or invasive (delicate needle-type electrodes that compensate for the thickness of the scalp). Tests detect the established pathways and the new pathways that are being created through activity (Miranda, 2015). Most EEG studies are conducted on individual children who engage with a play or learning activity, including their experience with screen technologies, and are detached from social context. This type of study does not allow for considering the interplay between children and their social environment – adults, siblings, and their peers – that behavioural observation noted was critical for learning. Researchers realized it was important to look at interactions that occurred in socially natural ways and with hyperscanning were able to record the neural activity of two (or more) individuals in naturalistic settings. Through DEEP, a dual electroencephalography analysis pipeline, they were able to create datasets which showed, for example, interaction between mother and infant (Kayhan, 2022).[6]

The MRI scanner, which uses magnetic resonance imaging to scan soft tissues such as the brain, heart, and muscles, was first used in 1977.[7] fMRI (functional magnetic resonance imaging), first used in 1991, showed that small changes in blood flow in certain parts of the brain occurred as a subject responded to a visual stimulus. Researchers could see what parts of the brain used energy when performing certain tasks. The MRI image is called functional because, unlike traditional MRI, they measure activity and how the brain performs tasks rather than showing the structure of the brain. fMRIs require immobility, but despite this drawback – children are not noted for their ability to stay still – this improvement in brain imaging technique provided opportunities to examine brain activity even in very young children and babies (Morita, 2016; Rosen, 2011). MRI research continued to respond to interest in improving the technology to understand cognition and in 1994 diffusion tensor imaging (DTI) was used to detect new pathways as they were being formed during learning experiences by showing fluid movement in white matter, the large network of nerve fibres or axons located under the cortex (grey matter) which connects neurons in the different regions of the brain (Fields, 2010; Qiu, 2015).[8] An example of what DTI studies can reveal is the difference noted in good readers and poor or non-readers in white matter in the temporo-parietal lobe (Feldman, 2010).[9]

What does brain research tell us that can be most useful to our study of representation in PEGI 3 and PEGI 7 games? Children's brains are wired to make connections and grow especially quickly; at around age three they contain more synapses that connect neurons than at any other time in children's lives. Then the brain begins to fine tune in order to make the neural network more efficient. It starts to keep connections that are used repeatedly and prune away those that aren't used at all. At around age ten, growth and pruning stabilize and then, at the end of adolescence, begin to reduce (Banich, 2011; Bransford, 2000; Bruer, 2002; Sylwester, 1995). There was an assumption that as this synaptic activity slowed as children moved towards pre-teen years and also as children began to take on behaviour which is more adult in nature, they must have matured cognitively. More research conducted with pre-teens and teens showed that, while the brain may have grown to adult size and outward behaviour may be similar, both the structure and function of the brain are in the process of constant change and development, and that peak synaptic density is staggered in different regions from birth for about 20 years. They may look like adults, but pre-teens and teens have brains that are very different from that of mature adults (Gogtay, 2004; Morita, 2016; Sowell, 2003). Research into the adolescent brain found a period of increased synaptic activity in the frontal lobe, which governs judgement and behaviour. Older children are as eager to experience new things as are their younger counterparts, but the white matter, mentioned earlier as the layer of nerve fibres (axons) that connect different parts of the brain, isn't fully connected yet in this area (and apparently not completely until the early 20s) and this accounts for the inconsistent behaviour adolescents display (Gogtay, 2004; Sisk, 2004).

The earlier discussion on schema showed how young children build a scaffold of information they rely on for interpreting their world and that representation can sway how they will understand disability at an older age. This is substantiated by looking at how synaptic activity works. When a positive representation of a disability is introduced in a PEGI 3 game (Lennie in *Geoffrey Goes to the Fair*) or a PEGI 7 game (Bentley in *Sly Cooper*), it happens when synaptic activity is most exuberant and can take advantage of the period when synapse clusters are forming. The repetitive activity inherent in interactive games reinforces the synapse cluster and helps avoid pruning. If children then play games with similar positive narratives about competent characters with different disabilities *(Beyond Eyes, Weakless, Moss)*, the cluster will link and include the different disabilities so that they are part of the cluster. Each time they encounter positive representation, the synaptic activity around this positive outlook expands, secures, and conserves it (Kastellakis & Poirazi, 2019). Unfortunately, the same thing happens for repeated play of games which represent disability as a liability.

Mirror Neurons

In their work on emotion and movement, art historian, David Freedberg, and psychobiologist, Vittorio Galese, identify the neuroprocessing which links image and emotion. They show that our empathetic response to images is one of embodied simulation: because of mirror neurons, we feel and experience what we see in the same brain centres as those involved in the action we are viewing (Freedberg 2007).

As artists have been able to engage people emotionally through painting and sculpture, photographers through photos, and filmmakers through movies, so video game developers have tapped into the ability of visual media to connect players to characters emotionally and draw them into the narrative.

It is worth repeating what has been recognized by those who create the aesthetics which draw us in and affect us,

> *The painting will move the soul of the beholder when the people painted there each clearly shows the movement of his own soul... we weep with the weeping, laugh with the laughing, and grieve with the grieving. These movements of the soul are known from the movements of the body.*
> Leon Battista Alberti (1404–72) (Alberti, 1991)

Referencing studies of mirror neuron systems and embodied simulation, Freedberg and Galese make the point that when people look at an image, rather than interpreting what is happening through a thinking process, the image goes directly to the part of the brain where the action happens. They reference first individuals who look at figurative paintings with strong emotional themes – Michelangelo's *Prisoners*, Goya's *Desastres de la Guerra* – who found themselves simulating the movement and emotion shown. They also found the same sense of bodily involvement was created by the physical marks that constitute abstract painting and which are the visible traces of the artist's goal-directed movements. The discovery of mirror neurons provided a neurobiological explanation for what had been recognized but unexplained, the power of image to evoke emotional response and empathy. The motor areas relevant to making the marks are activated in the viewer's brain. There is no interpretation, no considering what is happening, no memory involved; rather mirror neurons are able to identify the action and unconsciously activate the same emotions and physical reactions that doing the action would entail. The empathetic response is automatic and immediate.

Empathetic response tells us that when children see images these are not viewed objectively but rather intimately, and the player will experience a disability shown realistically with the same reactions, emotions, and feelings as the character experiences. How this sense of reality might play out in integrating representations into a child's schema of disability can be seen in the two games *Beyond Eyes* and *Pulse*. Both of these games show representation of blindness. *Beyond Eyes* is based in watercolour scenery that emerges in lyrical slowness and calm beauty. The player as the blind Rae moves forward with trepidation. She is hesitant as echolocation guides her into white, empty space that slowly changes colour for the player to see what Rae hears. The player controls every action and mirror neurons bring the player into the same space that Rae occupies. In *Pulse* Eva moves forward through a much more dramatically envisioned space, implying a darker and, at times, frightening experience of blindness. The aesthetic emerging from the echolocation is faster paced and dynamic, similar to that in a traditional adventure game. Eva is scared at times and mirror neurons play in that part of the player's brain where the action creates the same fear for them.

Indicative of the importance of mirror neurons and their association with imitating behaviour and learning new skills is the actual use of mental imagery for training stroke victims in which movement on one side of the body is affected. For a right hand which is disabled, a mirror is placed against the person's left hand. The left hand completes a series of movements which the brain sees in the mirror's reflection as the right hand. The mirror therapy influences the neural circuitry: the brain believes the right hand is moving and begins to reactivate the neurons associated with that movement.[10] "Studies hypothesize that mirror neurons provide a fundamental neural basis for building imitative skills" (Carvalho, 2013). The games children play in which they imitate behaviour assimilates the attitudes in the game which in turn influences children's own perception.

The behavioural and neurobiological research presented provides the fundamentals of child development that can now be brought to bear to frame children's experience with games in the next two chapters, first for representation of physical disability, and then representation of neurodevelopmental disability.

Notes

1 Vygotsky's research conducted in Russia from the 1930s was contemporary to Piaget's and Bruner's but was not substantially known in the West until it was made available in translation beginning with *Mind in Society* (1978).
2 Constructivism was brought to MIT in the 1960s by Seymour Papert who studied with Piaget in Geneva. It became the base for future development of educational children's games.
3 See Margaret Donaldson's *Children's Minds* for a discussion on context and the difficulty of asking the right questions when designing studies for children (Donaldson, 1978).
4 Narrative was also seen as basic to human understanding by Bruner (Bruner, 1991).
5 An extensive explanation with examples of these tools is available on Sue Lyle's Research Gate Site at https://www.researchgate.net/publication/259195198_romantic-understanding
6 Bright Minds Institute uses an enhanced EEG assessment, using 32 electrodes, which is also called DEEP. These are not related (Miranda, 2015).
7 MRI emerged from research into nuclear resonance imaging in the 1940s. History at https://www.researchgate.net/publication/288432025_A_short_history_of_magnetic_resonance_imaging
8 White matter is a relatively light colour because of the fatty myelin that surrounds the nerve fibres or axons. It sits beneath the grey cortex, or what is usually shown as the brain with its four different lobes: the frontal lobe, parietal lobe, temporal lobe, occipital lobe.
9 Other brain imaging techniques that provide measurements of brain activity without the use of invasive surgery include CT scans (based on X-rays), PET (uses short-lived radioactive material to track functional processes), MEG (measures magnetic fields), and NIRS (near-infrared spectroscopy). Brief explanations at http://psych-central.com/lib/types-of-brain-imaging-techniques/
10 This is a very simple explanation of a complex process which has been found to work on only some parts of the brain.

Works Cited

Alberti, L. B. (1991). *On painting* (C. E. Grayson, Ed.). London: Penguin.
Banich, M. T. (2011). *Cognitive neuroscience* (3rd ed.). Wadsworth: Cengage Learning.
Blunden, A. (2008, July). *Vygotsky's unfinished theory of child development*. Retrieved 2016, from Marxist Internet Archive: https://www.marxists.org/archive/vygotsky/works/comment/vygotsky-on-development.pdf
Blunden, A. (2011, February). *Vygotsky's theory of child development*. Retrieved from Andy Blunden on Vygotsky: https://www.ethicalpolitics.org/ablunden/works/vygotsky-development-mobile.htm
Bodrova, E., & Leong, D. J. (2015). Vygotskian and post-Vygotskian views on children's play. *American Journal of Play*, *7*(3), 371–388.
Bransford, J. D. (Ed.). (2000). *How people learn: Brain, mind, experience, and school.* Washington, DC: National Academy Press.

Bruer, J. T. (2002). *The myth of the first three years: A new understanding of early brain development and lifelong learning.* New York, NY: Free Press.

Bruner, J. (1991, Autumn). The narrative construction of reality. *Critical Inquiry, 18*(1), 1–21.

Carvalho D, T. S.-G.-C. (2013, October 17). The mirror neuron system in post-stroke rehabilitation. *International Archives of Medicine, 6*(41).

Donaldson, M. (1978). *Children's minds.* Flamingo.

Egan, K. (1997). *The educated mind: How cognitive tools shape our understanding.* Chicago, IL: University of Chicago Press.

Feldman, H. M.-B. (2010, May). Diffusion tensor imaging: A review for pediatric researchers and clinicians. *Journal of Developmental and Behavioral Pediatrics, 31*(4), 346–56.

Fettes, M. (2010). The TIEs that bind: How imagination grasps the world. In K.S. Madej and K. Egan (Eds.), *Understanding imagination and encouraging creativity in education.* Newcastle upon Tyne: Cambridge Scholars Press.

Fields, R. D. (2010, November 5). Change in the brain's white matter. *Science, 330*(6005), 768–769.

Freedberg, D. A. (2007). Movement, emotion and empathy in esthetic experience. *Trends in Cognitive Science, 11*(5), 197–203.

Gogtay, N. J. (2004, May 17). Dynamic mapping of human cortical development during childhood through early adulthood. *PNAS, 101*(21), 8174–8179.

Kayhan, E. (2022, April). DEEP: A dual EEG pipeline for developmental hyperscanning studies. *Developmental Cognitive Neuroscience, 54.*

Miranda, F. (2015). *Approach – EEP assessment.* Retrieved from Bright Minds Institute: http://www.brightmindsinstitute.com

Morita, T. A. (2016, September 15). Contribution of neuroimaging studies to understanding development of human cognitive brain functions. *Frontiers in Human Neuroscience, 10.*

Piaget, J. (1972). *The psychology of the child.* New York, NY: Basic Books.

Qiu, A. M. (2015, January). Diffusion tensor imaging for understanding brain development in early life. *Annual Review of Psychology, 66*, 853–876.

Rosen, B. (2011). *fMRI at 20: Has it changed the world?* Retrieved from Athinoula A. Martinos Center for Biomedical Imaging: https://www.nmr.mgh.harvard.edu/history/fmri-at-20

Sisk, C. F. (2004, October). The neural basis of puberty and adolescence. *Nature Neuroscience, 7*, 1040–1047.

Sowell, E. P. (2003, March). Mapping cortical change across the human life span. *Nature Neuroscience, 6*, 309–315.

Sylwester, R. (1995). *A celebration of neurons: An educator's guide to the human brain.* Alexandria, VA: Association for Supervision and Curriculum Development.

Tucker, D., & Luu, P. (2012). *Cognition and neural development.* New York, NY: Oxford University Press.

Vygotsky, L. (1978). *Mind in society: The development of higher psychological processes.* Cambridge, MA: Harvard University Press.

Wood, D. (1998). *How children think and learn* (2nd ed.). Oxford, UK: Blackwell Publishers.

4 The Games I, Representation of Physical Disability

Introduction

The behavioural and neurobiological research discussed in the previous chapters provides a broad picture of child development which recognizes the importance of children's early and middle years, from 3 to 10, in forming perceptions that last into adulthood. Together this chapter and Chapter 5 look at the representation of different types of disability in children's video games, correlate the representation with the cognitive abilities common to this development period, and briefly assess the type of representation it is. This chapter reviews games that show physical disability, Chapter 5 reviews games that show neurodevelopmental disabilities.[1] The original age categories for the study were young children, 3–5 or preschool, middle-age children, 6–8 or early elementary, older children, 9–11 or later elementary. These were set by reading ages and straddled the PEGI rating ages unnecessarily. The age categories have been reset to young children from 3–6, and middle years children 7–12, which is more consistent with PEGI 3 and PEGI 7 ratings. It should be noted that although the PEGI 7 rating is 7–12, because adolescence is considered to begin at 10 and it introduces a second period of neural exuberance with a different focus from the learning experienced by younger children to age 10, 10 might be a more appropriate age as an end bracket.[2] In the end, despite averages, it all depends on a child's individual experience.

The games industry, with over 3 billion players and at over 197 billion dollars worldwide, is considerable. WHO facts show that 16% of the world population or 1.6 billion people live with a disability. Children's games which include characters with disabilities are not plentiful. Popular games rated PEGI 3 are less so. The need to have more games to analyse motivated a search into historical games which included representation of disability. The search resulted in a list of educational and entertainment games which shows a marginal change through the 1980s and 1990s toward more inclusivity. Some of the games are no longer readily available and text descriptions are relied on (*Camp Frog Hollow*, 1996),[3] others have been documented by players with walkthrough or playthrough videos (*HunchBack*, 1983),[4] and some

DOI: 10.4324/9781003430445-4

are available to play through old game downloads and archives (*Winnie the Pooh, Preschool*, 1999).[5] Almost all of the PEGI 7 games, some over 20 years old, are currently available for play. Because of an increased discussion of diversity and inclusion in media and a greater awareness created by social media, developers of popular games are more often including characters with disabilities. In some, inclusion seems an afterthought, such as the birthday-girl-in-a-wheelchair in *Peg and Pog*, in others, the game is designed around the character's disability, such as the blind protagonist in *Pulse*. Educational game developers have also followed the trend and begun to include a diverse set of avatars for children to choose from in games such as *DreamBox Learning Math*. Cosmetic representation is typical across the entire spectrum of curriculum and grade-based educational games and only two such games (with different approaches) are included in the review.

Children's games which represent disability authentically are often developed by individuals with family, friends, or colleagues who have the disability, or organizations who advocate for inclusion and understanding. Small independent producers who create games that challenge the status quo now have opportunities, which were unavailable previously, to crowdfund development through GoFundMe, test and sell through Steam or Gog, and sell through avenues such as the Apple Store. As a result, games which would not have seen the light of day a decade ago are being brought to a public that is more regularly exposed to diversity by the media, and even (occasionally) expects it. Mentioned previously, Currys PC World study on Diversity in Gaming released in 2019, which looked at teen and adult games, noted that while the majority of disabilities portrayed are physical, since 2010 there has been an uptrend in representation of neurodevelopmental disabilities (Currys PC World, 2019). This trend is also visible in the study's PEGI 3 and PEGI 7 game lists.

The review revisits all the games chosen for discussion in the original research report. It also includes games that had been considered but not discussed as well as a number of games new to the author. Data is presented descriptively and narratively rather than quantitatively. While the games span a 40-year timeline beginning with the 1983 *HunchBack*, the analysis is not presented in time sequence. It looks at the most common physical disability represented in games, mobility, first, and continues with less-often represented disabilities such as blindness and deafness. It discusses games as cosmetic, incidental, and/or authentically representing the disability and looks at how the representation might influence perception given children's stages of development and their capacities and abilities (i.e. to cooperate). Different game genres, and within that each game, have mechanics and aesthetics (narratives, graphics) which are more easily referenced to certain aspects of development, for instance, arcade-style games can be discussed in light of stability and crisis because levelling up requires rapid mastery of skills. For the review this means each game is mapped differently and not always comparably.

A number of the games discussed in these two chapters have been used as examples or referenced in the child development chapters. In particular, the games, *Peg and Pog*, *Geoffrey at the Fair*, and *Backyard Baseball Junior* were examined in light of schema, and *Overcooked* and *Moving Out* in ratings. Only some of that discussion has been brought forward here.

Upper Mobility: The Wheelchair, an Iconic Symbol of Disability

Peg and Pog

The wheelchair has proven its convenience in representing disability in games in which it provides no real identification challenge and is used as dress or furniture in character or avatar design. A game for younger children in which a wheelchair plays such a cosmetic role is *Peg and Pog* (3–6), discussed in detail in Schema. This is a vocabulary-building game in which *Peg and Pog* (boy and girl) learn the names of objects during eight adventures, including on safari, shopping, and a final adventure at a birthday party. Four friends, one boy and three girls, one the birthday girl, join *Peg and Pog* at the party. The birthday girl uses a wheelchair and participates in all the group's activities, such as dancing and moving on and off stage, without exception. The mechanics are the same for all of the characters as they move across the space. The 2D graphics do show some body movements (arms swing, feet shuffle) but the girl does not manipulate the wheelchair nor do its wheels move. The scenario provides a player without any clue to the function or purpose of the wheelchair. Although this lack of information is due in part to the expedient use of 2D graphics and simple mechanics, simple solutions such as in *Geoffrey Goes to the Fair* in which Lennie uses a ramp and his friends the stairs, would have sufficed. The scenario does show, similar to Lennie's being part of a group of friends in *Geoffrey at the Fair*, that the girl is part of a group with whom she has fun and in which she is made to feel included. While Lennie's representation is more authentic, this cosmetic scenario can also advance important concepts of friendship that parallel young children's need to have supportive friends as they enter kindergarten. In addition, the girl is charmingly dressed and in a contemporary setting, which provides a positive reflection or mirror in which a child with a disability can see themselves. When children eventually learn what the wheelchair means, this simple message of friendship and positive reflection will have already gained some permanence through repetitive play.

The birthday girl in a wheelchair does not add to the story, does not change the game play, and does not add understanding of how a wheelchair is used, or what using one might mean to the birthday girl: this representation of a disability is a bare nod to inclusion. Even so, it needs to be considered bringing positive, negative, or neutral implications for a child's initial exposure to disability. Positive: being in a wheelchair is no big deal – a wheelchair user is considered to have the same capabilities as a non-wheelchair user. Negative: being in a wheelchair is no big deal – the actual difficulties of using a wheelchair are unimportant. Neutral: being in a wheelchair is no big deal – there is no discernible difference in ability. And this latter actually turns out to be a good perception to have.

Moving Out and Overcooked!

The 2D games *Moving Out* (PEGI 3), and *Overcooked!* (PEGI 7) are based on arcade action, with mechanics that are simple, but with game play that can become frantic as it consists of both multitasking and cooperative game play. Both games can be played as a traditional one- to four-player couch game, or with up to four players online. In *Moving Out* movers cooperate to move objects from a house into a moving van in a limited time. In *Overcooked!* chefs work together in busy kitchens to plate food and deliver it within a time limit. The games illustrate two common ways in which physical disability represented by a wheelchair is included in games. *Overcooked!* has many chefs (people, animals, and objects) to choose from for the cooking team, one of which, a racoon, is in a wheelchair.[6] *Moving Out* offers the option for any or all of the movers (people, animals, objects) on a team to be in a wheelchair, i.e. players can add it when they create their character.[7] In these two games the wheelchair appears as a cosmetic addition. If added, or chosen, it provides neither an advantage nor a disadvantage in play as the basic mechanics are the same for all the characters. In both games the wheelchair changes the aesthetics of play as it provides a visual of a character in a wheelchair, more so in *Moving Out* as the wheelchair is more distinct and the character turns the wheels to move about, providing some authenticity.

Implicit in the presence of the wheelchair is that it is a sufficiently recognizable symbol not to require an explanation. However, *Moving Out* is rated as a PEGI 3 game, and it may be that, as was discussed in Schema for the game *Peg and Pog*, also a PEGI 3 game, a younger player may not have seen a person in a wheelchair previously. There are important differences in the representation which influence how disability might be perceived. In *Peg and Pog* the birthday girl's wheelchair is fixed and given; the character does not require any input, does not seem to move differently in any significant way from the other characters, and does not seem to interact with the wheelchair. In *Moving Out*, the player must create the character and provide it with accessories, such as the wheelchair, which requires decision-making and a commitment to a position about including the wheelchair (or not). As an accessory, the wheelchair is shown in detail; there is first an implication that it has a purpose, and this implication is shown to be true when the character uses their hands to turn the wheels as they move about the game. Information is provided to begin to build a picture of the purpose of the wheelchair. In *Overcooked*, the Racoon Chef and wheelchair appear as one unit as does the birthday girl-with-a-wheelchair in *Peg and Pog*. He too doesn't need to use his hands to wheel around. The difference is that *Overcooked* is a PEGI 7 game, intended for children 7+, who are, more than likely, familiar with the wheelchair as a mobility aid.

Moving Out was designed with both accessibility and inclusiveness in mind. Developers referred to game accessibility guidelines to ensure they met, if not exceeded, best practices and added features such as an assist mode which allows players to slow game play, reduce difficulty, and add longer time limits.[8] As a PEGI 3 game, its accessibility features are a plus for younger children but may be beyond the capabilities of the youngest in this age rating. The accessibility features mean that there is a lower level of speed at which a player can gain mastery and advance in the game more easily. As they are working towards mastery, children find they can be equally successful when they choose a player in a wheelchair. Cooperative play is nascent in younger children, and for some, their entry into kindergarten is their first exposure to cooperative play, so the game is likely to be more successful as coop play with school-aged children (upper end of PEGI 3). In this situation too, children will find that their character being in a wheelchair does not impede success or add to it. As such, representation is cosmetic but important in its actual inclusion of a wheelchair user in the scenario.

Overcooked! in its original mode was difficult to master as the speed required to achieve success required a "frantic" pace that caused anxiety and frustration.[9] The cooperation required between players in two- to four-player mode, difficult even for adults, would have caused apprehension for middle years children as expectations for different parts of the task to be completed were unlikely to be met. There was no easy level and the game was not noted for any kind of accessibility until it was redesigned as *Overcooked: All you can eat* in 2020. The new edition was intended to be more family friendly. To do so, developers addressed issues which ranged from play that was too fast to flashing effects that could cause seizures and camera shake that caused motion sickness. There is more discussion of the game play (speed, complexity) for *Moving Out* and *Overcooked!* in Chapter 6: Ratings.

Curriculum-Based Educational Games: DreamBox Learning Math, Granny Prix

In keeping with the ongoing interest in educational games becoming more diverse and inclusive, the educational online site *DreamBox Learning Math* (5–9) includes different genders, races, and a symbol of physical disability, a wheelchair, in the avatar mix for its math and reading learning programmes. The DreamBox website states that such representation affects learning, "Because children learn best when they feel included and represented in the classroom."[10] Children choose an avatar and then go on to complete different math activities (games) similar to many that have been offered for the past four decades. Using an avatar in a wheelchair does not provide any information about the disability the character has. The mechanics and game play are the same whichever avatar is selected. The wheelchair is a positive cosmetic addition as it acts visually to be inclusive of players who are wheelchair users.

Granny Prix is an online set of math games (addition, multiplication) for children to practice quick recognition of addition and multiplication facts for grades K–8, as well as algebra, geometry, and pre-calculus. It is based on speed and children must answer questions quickly to win. They sign in, get to dress up granny and her wheelchair in fun ways, and are put together with three others to race by answering the addition or multiplication problems set at the top of the racecourse. The granny whose player answers the questions quickest wins. Why granny? Why a wheelchair? It is a spinoff of Grand Prix, and while showing a senior in a wheelchair is stereotypical ageism, no other name can replace and reference Grand as quickly and easily. The games put Grannies and wheelchairs in a positive light (although the Mohawk and Dreadlocks hair may be considered inappropriate), as the cosmetic representation of both is fun-loving and speedy. The use of wheelchairs is a marketing strategy which happens to provide cosmetic representational inclusivity.

Toca Life Series

The *Toca Life Series* is a long-running series of 2D sandbox games for children 4+ made for mobile technologies like smart phones and tablets. Among its collections of clothes and accessories it has glasses, prosthetic limbs, and wheelchairs. The first game in the series, *Toca Life: Town* (2014),[11] was followed by City, School, Farm, Stable, Hospital, Office, and others. Many of these were included in *Toca Life: World* which was released in 2018 and is available for free download. While advertised for 4+, it is on one hand recommended by parents for toddlers (3) and, on the other, played by many middle years and older children (even teens) who participate in the large Toca Boca online community through discussion, review, and by posting videos of their game stories.

Children can populate any of these worlds by choosing characters from a cast of over 300. The wheelchair collection includes a few different styles of wheelchair and many different colours to choose from. The game mechanics are very simple with flat, front-facing characters moving sideways or backwards and forwards. Objects float to where they are needed (toothpaste and toothbrush from the windowsill to the character's hand) and characters hop onto and off of beds, chairs, horses, and of course, wheelchairs, exactly the same way. It appears that all accessories are cosmetic, except that this is a sandbox game in which children create stories.

Children make up their own stories within a town, a hospital, or a farm and pretend play by moving the characters around the space with their finger. A player can add a wheelchair to every scene, or even two or three if they seem useful, as in, for instance, the hospital. Because the story is made up by the player, they can give the wheelchair whatever meaning they wish to. It can be decorative, just placed in the corner of a room, it can be cosmetic and used by a character to fool around in the scene without reference to actual purpose, as may happen with the younger children who are not familiar with the actual purpose of a wheelchair, or it can be part of a story in which the wheelchair is used in an incidental way. It can even be a part of a realistic, and modestly authentic scenario as demonstrated by the many videos of Toca Life stories with characters who break their leg accidently, get taken to the hospital for X-rays and a cast, and then are brought home with crutches and a wheelchair.[12] Such *Toca Life* stories are created using the sandbox game and are posted on the official YouTube Toca Boca channel as well as on personal YouTube channels by children who make videos of their game play.

There are many *Toca Life* stories that show wheelchair users as equally capable: typical is a morning routine which shows a little girl getting herself ready for school, helping her mother gather the breakfast dishes, and leaving with her brother who helps her by carrying her knapsack on his skateboard. At the request of players on the Toca Boca YouTube channel, one video was created to show a more complex scenario. The story is about a girl who dances and has an accident. It seems she will be unable to walk and must use a wheelchair. She's sad and encouraged to work hard at her physiotherapy so she can dance again. She completes her course of physio, is rehabilitated and able to dance, and is happy again. In this case the wheelchair represents loss and a disability that must be overcome. This is the prevalent social model of disability, someone has a problem that needs to be solved, or someone needs to be cured. When creating their own representation through sandbox games, children reinforce the perspective they play. Social media then plays its part in disseminating such stories widely as suggestions for others to play. In 2022 the Toca Boca YouTube channel[13] received 259 million views; it has a total of 1.6 million subscribers. Watching what children are saying to each other through these stories shows us the perception they have already formed of disability by the time they are pre-teens. While disability rights movements are beavering away to make gains, children are reinforcing existing stereotypes through stories they post on social media in ever increasing numbers.

As can be seen, the representation of disability in sandbox games does not fit neatly into a category such as "cosmetic" as there are gradations and variations in how each character is presented and because it is the player who creates the character and their story, representation is based in the player's past experience. It must be said that (1) the structure of the game, the basic mechanics, and the game graphics influence how the character is presented and received, (2) the game developers purpose influences how players are able to interact with the character, and (3) children's age, capabilities, and previous experience influences how they will perceive the representation with which they are interacting. There is no single outstanding item that will define how representation is perceived.

Animal Crossing, New Horizons

The life simulation game *Animal Crossing* was first introduced in 2001; *Animal Crossing, New Horizons*, the fifth in the series, was released in 2020 to much acclaim, winning many awards and was nominated for Game of the Year.[14] This Nintendo Switch game can be played by one and up to four players locally, and eight players online. The games are played in real time and the player takes on the role of a human who lives in village, a small town, or, in *New Horizons*, an uninhabited island. In the story, the player has purchased a tour package from Nook's Cranny to a deserted island where there are basic supplies such as a tent, light, camp bed, and Nookphone. The island is not completely deserted as it has two facilities, a Resident Services tent (like a village store), and an airport. In addition, two other characters have also bought packages and are on the island as companions. Players can customize (including design) every detail of their avatar (gender, dress) and their environment (trees, cars, and a wheelchair). They can fish, catch bugs, pick fruit, visit friends on other islands, and do yoga in their wheelchair.

Animal Crossing, New Horizons is easy to play and non-stressful, and it is not difficult to master. There is reading required so that children who do not read will need someone who does to guide them when they first start out. As in many games similar characters have identical dialogue, reading will not be as necessary as they progress in the game, although with any new character or situation, new dialogue is inevitable. Creating a simulated place to play fits into young children's interest in using objects in symbolically meaningful ways (i.e. creating a home with family) and their need to socialize and be autonomous (creating a village with people to interact with in activities they choose). The game offers both intrinsic and extrinsic rewards. Speaking with characters repetitively will eventually open up more dialogue but will also result in more tangible rewards, such as speaking to the character Sable will eventually open the design museum. Young children's instinctive use of repetition to learn new things will encourage such action and demonstrate to them that there's a tangible reward at the end of all that repetition. *New Horizon* has added NookMiles as rewards which can be collected slowly for just living on the island and more quickly for completing tasks. These can then be traded for many things like tools, recipes, travel (sound familiar?). Collecting is a tradition in video games (from points to stars) and fits into children's interest as they move from young to middle age.

The addition of a wheelchair as customizable houseware furniture in *New Horizons* was warmly welcomed by people who see inclusion of a wheelchair as a positive reflection of use of a wheelchair in regular daily life.[15] A limitation of the game is that vehicles, cars, bicycles, and this wheelchair, are not functional, they are only furniture. The wheelchair can be placed in different environments, someone sitting in it can exercise or do yoga, and it can be pushed around when it is empty, but not when a person is sitting in it.[16] As a representation of the function of the wheelchair, this is not authentic. However, as players can customize their character to look like themselves, they can also customize the wheelchair to look like their own as well, which add a personal component to the representation. As was posted on Reddit by one player, "Recreated my wheelchair, love that they included this in the game!"[17] The representation of the wheelchair as a personal item that creates both a physical and emotional attachment is authentic. *Animal Crossing* is well loved by teens and adults[18] and has been lauded as an excellent game for even the youngest children in the PEGI 3 rating, 3–6, to play. It is noted for being a safe, friendly, kind environment, where people share, help each other, form relationships, and create lasting friendships. Having a wheelchair in a game as positive as this one is envelopes the representation of disability in the game's qualities.

Last Day of June

The categories cosmetic, incidental, and authentic are crossed in the 3D adventure puzzle game *Last Day of June* (PEGI 7). In the game the protagonist, Carl, is driving home with his wife from an idyllic picnic at the lake; the car crashes, and his wife is killed. Carl is confined permanently to a wheelchair. We see him moving about his house and the representation seems authentic. The wheelchair is realistically depicted, Carl's hands turn the wheels to move through his house and manoeuvre around obstacles. He endures the difficulties that normally exist for a wheelchair user in a home, from getting a tin of food from a top cupboard shelf, to opening a door. These difficulties are portrayed in his actions and augmented by his voice as he audibly indicates how frustrating some actions are for someone unaccustomed to them. Being able to both see and hear him being frustrated adds to a player's ability to interpret Carl's frustration. The representation provides an accurate simulation of a person learning to use a wheelchair and in this way it is authentic. It is only incidental, however, and not instrumental to the story. The wheelchair represents the tragedy of the car crash and sadness for loss of a loved wife. It is not used symbolically to move the story forward, which is of revisiting memories through paintings, attempting to change past events, and eventually changing places with his wife in the car, saving her life along with that of their unborn child, and dying in her stead. It is not used physically to move the game forward, either. In the transition scenes, Carl is seen competently using his wheelchair to wheel from image to image both in the house and through imagined landscapes. But it wouldn't matter if he was walking rather than being in a wheelchair. The wheelchair, as it becomes second nature for Carl to use, is not shown as a hinderance, his disability, not something he must overcome or find a cure for. He is not stereotyped as someone to be pitied because of his disability. It is simply a part of who he is now.

This is a positive representation as Carl achieves his goal and important for children to see in a PEGI 7 game as they play his character. Carl's rages at not being able to master the shift in time and space so that he can make it work for his situation echoes the pattern of stability/crisis children themselves go through. Carl is trying to understand his new world and see how he fits in, he's testing the new shifts in time to see if he can change things. Children at this age are trying to understand the world and see how they fit in, to test their limits, see how they can push them. The puzzles Carl must work through on his road to figuring out his new world fit comfortably into the set of language tools children have learned to enjoy and like to solve. His increasingly skilful use of the wheelchair as the story progresses means it does not need to be compensated for as he faces challenges and solidifies the perception of competence children are building of disability through Carl's successes.

Sly 2: Band of Thieves and Sly 3: Honor Among Thieves

Sly Cooper (2002–2013) is a popular series of third-person platform stealth games which are noted for being family friendly and funny. The first two games *Sly Cooper and the Thievius Raccoonus* and *Sly 2: Band of Thieves* are rated PEGI 3,[19] while the next two games are rated PEGI 7. The ESRB rating is E. Two comic books, *The Adventures of Sly Cooper 1 & 2*, provide extra detail.[20] The story takes place in fictional versions of the real world and follows the adventures of master thief Sly Cooper, an anthropomorphic racoon, through various improbable capers. Sly has two partners, long-time friends, Bentley the turtle and Murray the hippopotamus, and a detective on their tail, Inspector Carmelita Fox. During the final battle at the end of the second game of the series, *Sly 2: Band of Thieves*, Bentley's legs are crushed by the enemy Clock-Lu's beak. The comic book, *The Adventures of Sly Cooper 2*, continues the story with Sly and Murray visiting Bentley in the hospital. Bentley has always been the brains and one of the reasons Sly and Murray go to the hospital is to ask him to help with plans for the next heist. He is in a wheelchair. They break him out and bring him back to their hideout, but his actual condition – is he paralyzed for life? could he be cured? – is not known. In the hideout, Bentley modifies his wheelchair and equips it with gadgets. *Sly 3: Honor Among Thieves* continues the story. He is still in a wheelchair after a year and it seems he will continue his life as a paraplegic, his wheelchair providing for the capabilities he has lost.

The disability and need to use a wheelchair appear as a symbol of Bentley's determination and ability to continue to help his friends. Part of the story wraps itself around what using a wheelchair means to a character in an action-oriented game. After he returned to the team, Murray, the brawn, said he would retire because he blamed himself for Bentley's accident. This was divulged in the comic so that the game *Sly: 3* began with Sly and Bentley going after Murray to get him to rejoin. The wheelchair adds both strengths and weaknesses: Bentley has added to his abilities by modifying his wheelchair to include moves and gadgets that are quite realistic – it can carry bombs which he throws, has a retractable pole with which he can pick pockets, and has a built-in dart gun. It can also spin super quickly and has jet engines, which are a little more of a superpower. But Bentley can no longer sneak across buildings or crawl in tight spaces and when he is separated from his wheelchair, his paraplegia makes him helpless, which are the reality of his kind of mobility disability. He is helped by his ingenuity and by his friends as when Murray saves him when he is knocked out of his wheelchair, and about to die at the hands of a deadly mobster in *Sly: 3*.[21]

Skills required for the first game are at the upper end of PEGI 3. As has happened in other game series, the first game is rated PEGI 3 but becomes progressively less appropriate for young children as action emulates adult behaviour or becomes more violent.[22] Of the four games, *Sly 2: Band of Thieves* is still rated PEGI 3. As children move from 3–6 to 7–12, their experiences of reality begin to move them towards differentiating between a dream world and reality. This game provides opportunities to see disability through a representation that while it is situated in a binary anthropomorphic world is also based in fact.[23] Bentley is a stand in for any person who has suffered an accident, he has to use a wheelchair, and is adapting because he's smart and is expected to adapt to the new situation. The wheelchair didn't make him smarter; it gives him the opportunity to apply his thinking to his situation. At a stage in their development when they are looking to explore their own limitations within the world around them, in Bentley, middle years children are exposed to a hero (not a supercrip) character who finds ways to successfully negotiate the world with a disability. In keeping with that age's interest in figuring out how to push boundaries, Bentley's work to make his wheelchair more than a standard issue one, and doing so fairly realistically through innovation, resonates with them.

As do many video game action-adventure narratives, the story negotiates between reality and fantasy. Bentley's story remains one of three stalwart friends, each being a helpful companion. Representation of disability is of determination and increasing confidence and skills in the face of odds. Bentley is not looking to be cured, not a victim, not a villain, and as for supercrip, he is, after all, a turtle in a fantasy game so a smidge of supering up his wheelchair should be expected. The representation is both incidental, the accident and ensuing disability begin new arcs in the story, and, instrumental, the wheelchair not only changes the way Bentley goes about business, but its use affects storyline (unlike *Last Day in June*). Representation is also modestly authentic, there is a hospital stay, a traditional wheelchair is supplied, the character looks to modify it to help him do what he wants to do, and while the wheelchair provides new ways to do things, it can't solve all his problems, either physical or emotional ones.

LEGO Marvel Super Heroes

Marvel superheroes have, between them, a wide range of physical and cognitive disabilities: mobility disability, ADHD, depression, blindness. In the comics and movies Professor X has a mobility disability and uses a wheelchair. In contrast, in the video game *Lego Marvel Super Heroes* (2013), he uses a hoverchair. Professor X does not have a wheelchair in the game that would allow switching between two mobility aids, the wheelchair and the hoverchair. The hoverchair is sufficiently unlike a wheelchair that it is no longer a reference to a disability (other than in the metanarrative) and, as a result, effectively erases Professor X's disability. Adding a wheelchair to Professor X's accessories as his means of getting around on the ground would have ensured a link between the disability and the hovercraft.

LEGO users have done just this. Fans have made wheelchairs for Professor X and provided suggestions and kits for making these chairs since 2013 when the game was issued.[24] LEGO added a wheelchair to its accessories in 2016 (although its Duplo sets have had a wheelchair since 2011).[25] A wheelchair accessory adds meaning to the hovercraft for children as they can exchange wheelchair for hoverchair and back. Bringing Professor X's disability into their pretend play by actively making him a wheelchair, and using it realistically, ensures children are involved in constructivist learning that creates a more accurate scaffold of information about why Professor X is using the hovercraft, i.e. he has difficulty with mobility. If only the hovercraft is used, the representation of disability is negligible.

Upper Mobility and the Prosthetic Hand

Lego Star Wars: The Skywalker Saga[26]

In the first Star Wars movie *Star Wars Episode IV: A New Hope* (1977), Luke Skywalker loses his hand in a fight with Darth Vader and it is replaced with a human-looking robot one. Sequences in the movie show doctor/technicians testing controls on the wrist and Skywalker flexing his fingers. In the later episodes the human-looking prosthetic is replaced with one which looks more robotic. Anakin Skywalker (later Darth Vader) also loses his hand – in a fight with Count Dooku in *Star Wars: Attack of the Clones*. In the action-adventure video game *Lego Star Wars: The Skywalker Saga* (2022), both of these scenes are replicated. The game is rated PEGI 7 in the UK and E10+ by ESRB in the US, although some US parents suggest that it is suitable for age 7 or even 5 and up, depending on the skill level of the child (it requires some skill in controlling the figures, and the ability to read is useful as there is text).[27] Adults who grew up with the films both watch the films and play the games with their children.[28]

The reviews indicate that while the story is fun for children to engage with, some skill is required, and if the game is introduced to children who do not yet have the necessary physical skills to manipulate characters, achieving mastery will include periods of frustration. Children as they move through their middle years are looking at the world around them and beginning to push boundaries. They are looking for heroes to show them the limits that are out there and who they can emulate. Luke Skywalker is such a hero. Despite his battle with Vader, despite losing his hand, he gets a new one and keeps on fighting. As well as providing a hero, *The Skywalker Saga* provides quite a number of slapstick antics and scatological humour that children find funny, a language tool they bring along with them from their interest in jokes and humour during their development of Mythic Understanding. Representation of disability shown through language that interests children is an effective way to get them thinking about the issue in ways they understand.

Today, the Star Wars story has a strong presence in popular culture and is considered a contemporary myth.[29] Robotics and social media make the myth a reality when movie hero Luke Skywalker/Mark Hamill tweets with 11-year-old Cameron Miller of Edinburgh (in 2019) and 11-year-old Bella Tadlock, from Tallahassee, Florida (in 2020), both Star Wars fans, who have been fitted with prosthetic arms that are modelled to look like those in *Star Wars*.[30] As social media brings stories together from across genres – film, games, and social media work together to link the representation of disability in the Star Wars stories to real life and authenticate the hero in the fantasy story. It is much more difficult today to give up the middle ground between real and unreal that getting older requires when the world around us begins to emulate the world in fantasy. Robotically enhanced humans aren't only possible, they exist, bringing a new twist to the definition of people with different capabilities.

Blindness, Deafness

Beyond Eyes and Pulse

How can blindness be represented in a game to show what it is like to not be able to see? *Beyond Eyes* and *Pulse* are two games which use echolocation (*Pulse* developers say the game uses sonar, similar to echolocation) to draw players into the game through visual metaphor. In both these games a visible environment is revealed to the player in simulation of what the blind protagonists "sees" as they move forward by localizing sounds, and the echoes of these sounds, to a specific area. In both games, the protagonist became blind through an accident and has memories of what the world looks like. The games have unique approaches that result in different quality and tone and provoke very different responses.

Beyond Eyes (PEGI 3)

Beyond Eyes[31] has been included in the genre known as "walking simulator," a game in which the protagonist walks through the story. Rae, a young girl of 10, has recently had an accident caused by fireworks at a celebration she was attending. She is seen in a hospital bed with bandages on her eyes, and then, two juxtaposing vignettes show friends playing in a playground and Rae sitting on a bench in her garden. Her head is hung low in sadness and this demeaner is a symbolic of the loss of her sight (her head is hung low through most of her walk). The text commentary tells us Ray has spent quite a bit of time on her own. As the scene around Rae is completely filled with lyrical watercolours, she is visited by a friendly ginger cat. After a moment of petting, the cat jumps from the bench and heads down the path. Rae gets up, follows, and becomes friends with "Nani" as they explore the garden together. Rae worries each time Nani leaves the garden that she won't come back. One day she doesn't. Rae misses her friend and leaves the garden, her known space, to find her.

The scene as Rae first leaves her bench and looks to the wider space around her has large swaths of white (i.e. it is empty) and is watercoloured only immediately around Rae. As she moves forward the scene fills in bit by bit. Rae uses touch and sound, both what she feels (the ground beneath her feet, the fence) and hears (birds, water fountain), to find her way and as she walks towards the sounds, the emptiness is populated with flowers, grass, trees, a path, a fountain – that then remain visible. What she has heard and felt and turned into imagery persists in memory and does not disappear. Sounds that are far away, such as a bird twittering or a cow mooing, appear only momentarily and partially until they are within Rae's echolocation distance, then they are permanent. For the game player there are some puzzles and achievements.[32] Puzzles are simple things like figuring out how to turn the street caution light on so she can cross the street safely. Achievements are challenges included by the developer to provide the impetus for the player to find all of the game's secrets and complete all of its challenges. In *Beyond Eyes* there are ten which have the player sharing Rae's emotional experience. The first time that Rae picks flowers for the cow, she drops them as the mooing scares her; if the player has Rae pick the flowers again and bring them to the cow, the cow moos, chomps on them, and Rae gives a little giggle. The achievements in order are as follows:

- Courage, Feed the cow by hand
- Persistence, Get a chicken across the bridge
- Lonely, Sit on the swing

- Bravery, Overcome your fear of the dog
- Adventure, Follow and free the flower
- Thoughtful, Feed the ducks
- Attraction, Collect all five butterflies
- Imagination, Find all Nani experiences
- Truth, Discover everything's true identity
- Closure, Complete the journey

Rae's movement forward is steady but quite slow, the clomp, clomp of her feet quiet or loud without reference to the surface she is walking on (this is a bit unsettling). It is this sense of slowness and hesitancy, and the need for repeated forays into spaces to make them appear, that seems the essence of the caution someone newly blind would feel. Another reflection of blindness is the gap between the remembered and the reality. Rae hears what appears in the distance to be clothes flapping on a line but on coming closer the sound is a scarecrow. You can see her surprise and fear. This is a Truth. There are many Truths in the game as they are one way to show the difficulty in knowing from sound what something might actually be. Some resolve quickly, the fountain is really a drain, but others, like the scarecrow, take some time as they may be further away.[33] The representation of blindness is both incidental in that it causes the events in the game, as well as instrumental as the blindness is a factor throughout the game. It also seems to be authentic in how it shows echolocation can work, how courage may be required and happen, and how sounds can be deceptive. The game's reception has been positive, and the representation in the game has increased awareness in a positive way for adults as well as children.

While *Beyond Eyes* is rated PEGI 3, the designers are encouraging empathy in an abstract way, within what is more an experience than a story, and which is likely to be missed by younger children. Although they will get the point of missing Nani, this may be a moot point as they may never get to where she is missing in the game because there is no story to follow. The game's representation of disability will resonate more strongly with middle years (7+) children who are testing the world around them and pushing its boundaries. A blind girl who uses echolocation to find her way corresponds to older children's interest in experimenting with different ways of being in the world. Knowing that there are truths and achievements to find will encourage playing the game to the end. The authenticity mentioned above: how courage may be required, along with the other achievements such as persistence and bravery, are ideas that children are capable of understanding and fitting into a positive view of disability.

Pulse (PEGI 7)

The game *Pulse* is bolder and more strident in its approach to visual references of a blind experience than is *Beyond Eyes*. *Pulse* is a survival story of Eva, who lost her sight in her childhood, and lives a protected life until she follows her brother Tahu to save their land. She uses a type of sonar to find her way and can only see what she can hear. This means the player can only see what is revealed directly ahead of them as they move forward as Eva. The sonar waves create wooden boardwalk steps, flowered forest floors, and rock pathways as Eva steps on them; at times wavery lines signify sound waves across the scene. When Eva stops walking and no sounds vibrate, all is black. Most notable about Eva's path is that as it progresses, the scenes become chaotic and confusing. The sounds of Eva's footsteps together with the forest sounds, the reverberating sounds of the sonar, and Eva's breathing create dissonance and add to the growing sense of apprehension. The space is difficult to inhabit both cognitively and emotionally as the player tries to make sense of the space to navigate it.

There seems little story to provide context for where Eva is going or to evoke a personal engagement with her, as no information is provided about how she went blind, or about her people, her village, or the menace she will be fighting. The forest she initially enters loses its character, which can enhance a story when there is a purpose for the change, but there seems no reason other than it begins to appear menacing. For children this then becomes just a game, not a game with a story to share and with which to become engaged. The representation of blindness is not incidental, it doesn't set what little story there is on its way, Tahu's disappearance does. Representation of blindness is instrumental as all of the action is said to be based on Eva being blind and using her sonar ability to find her way, although it is difficult at times to see that she does this. There are oddities in the environment that don't seem to fit graphically and also have no context, such as the stark image of the raven (crow), and the round white forest sprites, the Mokos. Neither seems related to either the story or to being blind. Even though the Mokos are intended to provide extra sounds to clarify the space when it is confusing, they can be difficult to direct and can end up being simply cutesy creatures dashing about without any rationale.

The game is rated PEGI 7 but 13+ by Common Sense Media. This discrepancy reflects how experiencing a first-person visual and sound environment can appear menacing to some and not to others. The game play, which is initially intuitive, and simple to master, becomes increasingly difficult so that mastery becomes difficult to achieve, even for older children. This is particularly true when there are no consistency in the clues to guide the way and repetition does not seem to achieve mastery. The ensuing frustration might negate any positive view of a blind person competently moving through the world. The implication is that they are more often frustrated than able. This confusion of figuring out or recognizing where to go next, especially figuring out why a certain route works, and the cacophony of images and sound that occasionally occurs, seems to provide a representation of people who are blind as living in a very confusing and alarming world and needing help, a representation that is stereotypical. The player as Eva does move through some of the environment competently using sonar, and that is positive representation. Middle years children would find the sonar location a phenomenon interesting to experience and about which to find out more. Context in the shape of having some background about how Eva learned to do this would go a long way in engaging players more personally with the character and her disability.

A last word about these two games, and about the reviews that have been written about them. *Beyond Eyes* received many reviews which noted its beauty, lack of story, and nobleness of intent. *Pulse* received reviews which noted its good old-fashioned platforming moves, lack of story, and nobleness of intent. Typical is the following comment in a *Pulse* review, "I see what the developers were aiming for here – an artistic representation of the struggles of sensory impairment – but the result leans much more towards frustration than enlightenment" (Sullivan, 2015). There are two points to make here. First, reviewers should rate the game fairly and not apologize for having to give a game a bad review because it shows a representation of a character with a disability in an experimental way (of course they can give it kudos for being experimental); the game may actually stand in the way of authentic and meaningful representation. Second, reviewers are continuing to identify people with disabilities as "struggling," a social model they should be aware disability rights groups are working to change.

Weakless

Weakless is a puzzle adventure game that brings players the story of two tree-like creatures, Weavelings, who set out to save their planet from a poisonous fog.[34] The Blind One and The Deaf One work together in collaboration to take advantage of each one's strengths to complete puzzles and manoeuvre successfully through the game. The Blind One is tall and calm, has a scarf around its eyes, and many branches which glow at their ends growing from its head. It can only sense its immediate space and it carries a staff which when tapped on the ground makes more of a black and white environment visible. It is very strong and uses its strength to move objects like platforms to help The Deaf One get from place to place. It is a musician and tries the musical instruments found on the journey. The Deaf One is a short child-like Weaveling, with a backpack, whose head branches have been twisted in a topknot to create a bobbing, glowing orb of light which it uses to light up new places. It is a painter and carries a painting journal in a backpack. It is painting everything around him that got the Deaf One sent out of the village when it met The Blind One. The two became friends and fellow adventurers. The painting journal is consistently referred to and helps the friends decide what something is and/ or which way to go, so they can address puzzles that need to be completed.

When playing The Blind One, the world is filled with melodies, but the environment is black, white, and grey. When playing The Deaf One, the world is filled with vibrant colours, but the sound is muted. The switch is constant as the player controls each of the Weavelings alternatively to move forward. This contrast and switch in imagery, black/white vs colour, is a continuously present reminder of the nature of the Weavelings respective disability. Each Weaveling has its abilities and can only undertake certain types of action. The Blind one can tap its cane on the ground to extend how far it can "see" its environment and it can push things to help them get access to difficult places. It also activates sound-based switches. The Deaf One can activate switches that are visible and produce its painting journal when needed. The colour use and the related cause-and-effect mechanics that are a part of each character's identity fit into children's ability to mentally represent and remember these mechanics and apply them to the next puzzle. The steady pace of and consistency in the game action makes mastery achievable without much frustration and once young children learn what each Weaveling can do through repetition, they are able to negotiate future events. Players must learn to switch back and forth between the Weavelings as puzzles may require more than one set of skills and some collaboration to make things happen. This switching may be more difficult for the youngest in the age group but as a skill, it can be learned with repetition. The collaboration comes more easily as children reach their middle years, when children become more socially aware, are beginning to work with others, and are learning to collaborate.

After playing within one world even for a short time, the sense being used (i.e. practised) is heightened. When the player switches from colour to black and white, or from full to muted sound, that difference is starker and better noticed after practice. As children move into middle years, they will be interested in comparing the two and even experimenting with the effects. Representation of the two disabilities working together provides a more accurate portrayal of each, shows to advantage how senses are heightened, and encourages a positive approach to working together as a team while using individual abilities to benefit a quest. The obvious friendship that exists and the reliance on each other that the Weavelings demonstrate by helping each other works to engage children in a supportive social environment and also to engage them emotionally with the characters. Close to the end of the story, The Blind One puts its arm around a tired and drooping Deaf One to help it down the path. Working together the two characters finish their quest by removing the rotting pipes in the Bastian Tree and save their world. The representation of disability shows the advantages of the skills each character has, the disadvantage of originally being outcasts in the village, and the counterbalance of their ability to achieve their goal of saving it together.

The representation of each disability is incidental to the story. It is the disability of each character which has forced it from the village so that they would find each other. It is also instrumental in moving the story forward as the game is designed around puzzles that only the particular ability can achieve. As a fantasy adventure its representation of the reliance of two characters with different disabilities on each other is intriguing and heartwarming.

Moss – Virtual Reality

New immersive technologies such as augmented and virtual reality are noted for their ability to create a sense of really being in a place. In games they offer a realistic experience that brings an intimate sense of engagement with a character. VR headsets such as Oculus Quest 2 and PSVR are recommended only for children over 12 because of potential issues with their neural, visual, and physical development. Despite this recommendation, headsets are being designed for children ages 5–12 because of their ability to engage. Parental sites make recommendations for purchasing VR gear for children and technology experts say children's use is inevitable.[35] Because of the newness of the technology, very little testing has been done to date and organizations such as Vision Fountain make their VR culture experiences for players 10 and up.[36] One of the challenges of keeping children safe in a household in which older siblings and parents play games has been the spillover effect. Current age recommendations notwithstanding, 10-year-olds and younger children as well, will be around when the family plays games and will use a sibling's or parent's headset to join the game. With that in mind, we will look briefly at the VR game *Moss*, an action-adventure puzzle game rated PEGI 7 and E. The game features protagonist Quill, an adventurous mouse who has become a positive symbol of inclusion since emerging on the scene in 2018 in *Moss: Book I*. While not deaf, Quill can only squeak and in her initial design relied on gestures and pantomime to communicate. The animation director wanted her to be able to communicate more clearly and tested the idea of using American Sign Language.[37] Her use of American Sign Language to communicate (even though this is not often) together with her engaging personality strikes a chord in players. The game has been noted for its ASM realism by deaf and hoh (hard of hearing) players in their reviews as a welcome representation of deafness in the industry.[38]

Quill's task is that of a traditional hero: she must save her uncle who has been captured by the fire-breathing snake Sarffog. In the game, the point of view is player as reader, and scenes unfold as pages of the book turn. The player acts as Quill's protector and VR gives them the opportunity to get close to Quill, personally make her healthy again when she has suffered a hit, pet her when she's tired, and read what she says as she signs. There is never any danger to the reader, and they never interact with anyone else in the story. This personal engagement with the endearing mouse, and the opportunity to see her using sign language as a hero in this adventure game, makes for a representation of the disability that is positive and enabling. The sequel, *Moss: Book II*, takes up where the first game ended. Quill has saved her uncle, but her world still needs saving. The reader is given some agency in the action (make vines, destroy objects) and the point of view is now from Quill's perspective so many details can be experienced from a mouse's size. Quill continues to sign to communicate and this, together with her hero quest, makes *Moss* an ideal narrative for middle years children who want to explore new worlds with their heroes. The signing is authentic while not incidental or instrumental, and the representation creates a positive schema of deafness, even though Moss is not deaf herself, because it affirms the use of ASL as an important communication tool.

Asthma

Buster Baxter: Lung Defender

Buster Baxter: Lung Defender is a short PBS online educational game which introduces children to common triggers of asthma. Health problems such as asthma are not often seen in arcade action games but the presentation of disability in this one, if basic, is factual. The game is based on *Buster's Breathless*, an episode in the fourth season of the popular children's PBS television series *Arthur*. Children who watch PBS would be familiar with Buster and the difficulties he has with activities such as playing outdoor games. Buster is seen as a typical kid; children watching the program may have asthma or have a friend who does, which would provide incentive for them to learn about what causes it. The game shows triggers (cigarette smoke, cat dander) and shows what the triggers do physically (narrow breathing passageways). Game mechanics are very simple, suitable for the youngest of PEGI 3 players.

At the beginning of the game, Buster says he has asthma and that means there are certain things in the air (triggers) that make it hard for him to breath. A ship flies into Buster's lungs to help catch some of these bad triggers and prevent an asthma attack. A scrolling graphic, like a conveyer belt, which represents Buster's air passageway appears and is soon populated by a few mites. The player is supposed to zap them by clicking on them using a mouse or keyboard. The mites appear more and more quickly. If not enough mites are caught, the lungs constrict, and an inhaler appears. Children can click on the inhaler which then provides a puff that opens up the lungs again. The game is simple, with few mechanics, and is easy to play, although as mites increase and the conveyer belt speeds up, mastering the skill needed to zap them may require a young child several repetitions. The game offers children a small amount of agency in controlling the mites with the inhaler but there is no situational context which connects the arcade graphics of the lungs to the problems caused in everyday life by the condition, such as difficulty breathing when inhaling too much dust. Because the game is a spin-off of the television program, this connection must have seemed sufficient reason for not providing such contextual information. But even when it was first released, context would have added to the authenticity of the representation. At this point, the disability is not represented, only a person's air passage is. A child watching the program has no reference that links the images in the game to a person/character who is suffering an asthma attack on being exposed to a trigger and being helped by an inhaler. It can only be representative when used in conjunction with other materials in an educational program.

Familiar Story Characters

One set of games which is often forgotten but which has been important in adding to how young children view disability is those based on familiar children's story characters who have a disability and who have been introduced by books, television, or movies. Early games include examples such as *HunchBack* (1983) published for the BBC Computer Literacy Project and *Peter Pan, the Adventure Game* (1984) published by the print publisher Hodder & Stoughton. Young children, who have first encountered these characters in books, television, and movies, have a view of the character which is cumulatively based on the representations in the different media.

HunchBack

Early games that were 2D sidescrollers such as *Hunchback* (1983)[39] have side-scrolling action with little story and minimum resolution in their graphics. The original game was an arcade game with better graphics but similar mechanics. Quasimodo must save Esmerelda and is dressed in green (because it seems the original game was planned to be about Robin Hood) and has a small hump on his back. Only players who know the story from books are likely to recall the character as having a disability. Quasimodo has to get to the end of the wall (far right of screen) dodging fireballs and arrows and swinging on a rope to ring a bell. Once he has completed a number of screens, he must save Esmerelda at which point the game starts again at a faster speed. Intended for younger children, mastery is gained through repetitive play. This is a very common type of sidescroller and children would bring skills from previous play to this one. Quasimodo's prowess at getting about Notre Dame (or this English castle) is proven each time the bell is rung, and his ability to scale walls and jump over objects in the game is a positive representation of someone with such a disability being quite capable and athletic. Any social stigma would not be visible in the game play and would be mitigated by hero status for saving Esmerelda. This representation is cosmetic at its most basic.

Peter Pan, A Story Painting Adventure

The *Peter Pan* stories are well known and in all of the games[40] the villainous, and comic, Captain Hook has a hook instead of a hand. He uses the hook very adroitly to aid him in his actions, from pointing threateningly with it, to hanging on to rigging as he is fighting. It is an obvious part of him, and although he comments on missing his hand, he uses the hook to advantage to do many things. It is a representation of both a lost limb and of his villainousness. Even when seen as an object (jacketed arm with a hook at the end), as in the introductory credits to *A Story Painting Adventure*, it is a representation of Captain Hook rather than of a disability. The hook is a source of anxiety for the Captain. He is anxious when he hears a clock tick because of the circumstances of losing his hand. The alligator, which is said to have swallowed his hand when it was cut off by Peter, has also swallowed a clock, which can be heard as the alligator continues to search for the delectable Captain. Peter teases Captain Hook by putting his hand up to his ear and saying, "is that a clock ticking?" The Captain's anxiety is treated in a comic fashion, but it is, nevertheless, anxiety, and Peter teases and bullies him about it. The original book and theatrical presentation were for adults, although it soon became popular with children, but the animated version created in the 1950s by Disney and the games that were created from the 1980s on were intended for young and middle years children. The representation of disability in these games associates the physical disability stereotypically with villainy and encourages negation of the anxiety associated with the event that caused the disability by mocking it with the sound of a ticking clock.[41]

Finding Nemo

Anthropomorphic animals are well suited to act as metaphors which make it easier for children, and adults as well, to grasp concepts. Many animated films made for children have concepts built into the story such as be kind, be courageous, and help others, which are reflected in how the characters conduct themselves. This didacticism is long standing in stories written for children and most Disney-animated films from the last 25 years have characters learning a lesson from their experiences.

In the very popular film *Finding Nemo* (2003), the film's protagonist is a little clownfish named Nemo. In the opening scene of the movie, two clownfish, Marlin and Coral are enjoying their new home and talking about the 400 children they will soon have. A shark attack puts an end to their dreams. When Marlin wakes from being knocked out, only one little fish egg has survived the onslaught. It has a small crack and Marlin vows to take care of it. That egg hatches to be Nemo and six years later (after the opening title credits) Marlin is taking Nemo for his first day of school. Marlin is very protective and asks the teacher, Mr. Ray, to take care of him, explaining about the shorter fin.[42] He explains to Nemo's friends that "he was born with it, it's called his lucky fin."[43] Pearl, a little octopus, pipes in that she has one shorter tentacle, and Sheldon, the seahorse, says he is H20 intolerant. Nemo and Nemo's friends do not see his shorter fin as a disability. Only his father does.

Finding Nemo generated a number of video games.[44] Most are arcade-style games in which the fin is shown smaller but have no explanation for it being that way and game play does not change because it is smaller. In

Finding Nemo (2003), a video game which has more narrative, Nemo's dad is constantly asking if his fin is ok, and Nemo shows disdain for these comments with rolling eyes as he is able to complete all the tasks in the games easily. To Nemo, while his fin might be different it is not a disability. The representation of the excessive overprotective father results in Nemo diving down deep into the ocean to the "butt" to show he can. This reflects the same need to be autonomous shown by children throughout their development. In the game, Nemo completes all tasks until he needs to escape from the tank in the dentist's office. In the game he is given training to use his fin more effectively by Gill before his second, more successful escape. The representation is of learning to use the fin to advantage in a challenging situation, similar to training for the Olympics; it is not a loss of ability. The disability is incidental to the training scene and instigates a rerun of the escape, which is successful.

The next section, on Neurodevelopmental Disability, continues the discussion of representation with Nemo's friend Dory, who is noted for her memory loss.

Notes

1 Thanks to improvements in neurobiological technology, and as neurobiological and mental health disorders are receiving more attention, they are being redefined. The term neurodevelopmental is currently seen as implying "an early origin and a neurobiological correlate, in the establishment of which aversive events during gestation or at birth often play a role" (Cainelli, 2022).

2 The World Health Organizations considers children aged 10 and above adolescents, see at https://www.who.int/health-topics/adolescent-health#tab=tab_1. At puberty children enter into a new neural development period during which the amygdala that is responsible for immediate reactions develops early but the frontal cortex that controls reasoning and helps us think before we act, develops later.

3 There is an original CD of *Camp Frog Hollow* at the Strong National Museum of Play in Rochester, New York, US.

4 *HunchBack* playthrough at https://www.youtube.com/watch?v=nWSLCkGGgoU. There is a downloadable dos version at https://www.myabandonware.com/game/hunchback-2h8

5 Old Game Downloads, play at https://oldgamesdownload.com/disneys-winnie-the-pooh-preschool/

6 Animals have been used as metaphors for people in myths, fables, and fairytales for centuries. Anthropomorphism became well established through animated films in the 20th century and continues its presence in narratives as a metaphor for human action in all media.

7 https://www.vg247.com/moving-couch-co-op-wheelchairs-hijabs

8 *Moving Out* developers commented they were influenced by game developer Jan Rigerl who previously released a game called *Extreme Wheelchairing* "He had a lot of great feedback from people in wheelchairs saying that the game is really fun and it's great that they get to look like the hero and thanking him for giving them that opportunity." See at https://powerup-gaming.com/2020/03/18/moving-outs-accessibility-options-and-inclusivity-set-a-new-standard/. For the developer's commitment to creating an accessible and inclusive game, see also stories at https://www.gamesradar.com/moving-out-developer-talks-accessibility-we-want-everyone-to-

be-able-to-finish-it-and-everyone-to-be-able-to-play/ and https://www.gamespot. com/articles/moving-out-dev-on-the-importance-of-inclusivity-an/1100-6477261/

9 *I Can't Convince My Friends That Overcooked 2 Is Fun, Not Stressful*, https://kotaku.com/i-cant-convince-my-friends-that-overcooked-2-is-fun-no-1837838614

10 https://www.dreambox.com/resources/blogs/bringing-diversity-and-inclusion-to-math-classrooms

11 Toca Boca has been making award winning children's games since 2011.

12 An example is *Andrea Broke Her Leg*: https://www.youtube.com/watch?v=Z7 gebM4D_4k

13 The YouTube channel is intended for children 6–14, https://hr.linkedin.com/ posts/toca-boca_we-were-recently-invited-to-the-youtube-awards-activity-7009517628545241088-IL1C. YouTube Channel at https://www.youtube.com/@ tocaboca.

14 As a PEGI 3 game, statistics for its appeal are impressive, grossing an estimated $2 billion in its first year as of March 2021. In 2020, it was the year's best-selling game in Japan, second best-selling game in the UK, and third best-selling game in the US, https://www.gamesindustry.biz/gamesindustry-biz-presents-the-year-in-numbers-2020

15 https://kotaku.com/i-m-so-happy-there-s-a-wheelchair-in-animal-crossing-n-1842492728, https://www.facebook.com/SPINALpedia/posts/a-wheelchair-is-now-featured-in-the-popular-video-game-animal-crossings-new-hori/ 10158423875079235/

16 A petition has been started to make the wheelchair useable, but as this would take a change in mechanics, it is unlikely it will happen. https://www.change.org/p/ nintendo-dear-nintendo-please-make-the-wheelchair-usable-in-acnh

17 https://www.reddit.com/r/AnimalCrossing/comments/i0oooe/recreated_ my_wheelchair_love_that_they_included/

18 https://www.nytimes.com/2020/06/17/learning/how-animal-crossing-will-save-gen-z.html, https://www.sciencefocus.com/news/why-are-so-many-people-playing-animal-crossing/

19 The first game was re-rated PEGI 7. Parental comments at https://www.imdb.com/ title/tt0354920/parentalguide/#advisory-violence

20 The entire storyline as it includes Bentley is available at https://slycooper.fandom. com/wiki/Bentley

21 For complete information on Bentley's wheelchair see https://slycooper.fandom. com/wiki/Bentley%27s_wheelchair

22 It is also interesting to note that *Sly 2: Band of Thieves* has remained a PEGI 3 game, while the first game *Sly Cooper and the Thievius Raccoonus h*as been rerated to PEGI 7. Violence and sex, which seemed appropriate 20 years ago, have been reevaluated as none (1) or mild (3). Comments include: "One of the enemies in the game is a cartoonish giant mosquito, which can kill Sly by sucking his blood and squirting it out. Naturally, a huge amount of blood is seen, but the blood is purple and not red, for some reason (probably to keep the game rated E)" and "Carmelita's outfit includes a shoulder less top that exposes her midriff."

23 This is true of many anthropomorphic movies and games, as anthropomorphism is most often used as a metaphor for human behaviour.

24 Professor X in wheelchair, custom built at https://www.eurobricks.com/forum/index. php?/forums/topic/84980-moc-professor-x/, https://rebrickable.com/mocs/MOC-52138/g.lego.customs/wheelchair-professor-

25 LEGO has included wheelchairs in its sets over the years: in 1995 the Dacta Control Lab Building Set included a joystick-controlled wheelchair, in 2011, Duplo offered a single-mould wheelchair, in 2015 Duplo released a senior citizen in a wheelchair (how stereotypical!) as part of their Community People Set, and in 2016, LEGO released a wheelchair as part of its Fun in the Park set.

26 Captain Hook (*Peter Pan*), who has a hook as a prosthetic replacement for his hand, is discussed in the section Familiar Story Characters.

27 Opinions differ: All quotes from https://www.commonsensemedia.org/game-reviews/lego-star-wars-the-complete-saga/user-reviews/adult

10+ "Battles are frenetic, accompanied by laser-fire effects, explosions, and cries of pain. The game also includes protracted one-on-one boss battles with Star Wars villains. In one sequence, a pile of Lego studs resembling feces can be seen next to a janitor."

5+ "IT'S ALL LEGO. Violence? ITS LEGO! WHEN PEOPLE DIE THEY RESPAWN WITHOUT LOSING ANYTHING! Sex? please. NOTHING! the problem Is that it's hard to play u need to be precise with the controls."

5+ "My 4 year old after having beat all of the Dora/ Diego type games in no time, was bored with little kid games. So he and my husband play the Lego games, Little Big Planets and Kirby Yarn games. He really enjoys them and one of us always play with him. We also talk about how these characters are Lego figurines and just break apart and can be put back together (and how this isn't how it is for real people). We also talk about how we aren't killing we are breaking them apart or blowing them apart. We won't let him watch the StarWars movies for several more years but we love this game. Great family fun!"

28 David Kender provides an extensive guide to what part of the different film episodes might not be age-appropriate at https://reviewed.usatoday.com/televisions/features/star-wars-whats-the-right-age-to-watch-the-movies. He says, "Most parents – at least those who, like me, are inordinately attached to *Star Wars* – felt that around four to seven years old was the sweet spot. At that age, most children have sufficient attention span to sit down and follow a feature-length story."

29 Popular culture studies include discussions on the evolution of the Star Wars Myth (Henderson, 1997).

30 https://deadline.com/2019/03/mark-hamill-makes-kids-light-year-with-tweet-about-boys-bb-8-bionic-arm-1202581222/, https://www.dailymail.co.uk/news/article-8067655/Girl-11-receives-R2-D2-bionic-arm-phone-call-Mark-Hamill.html

31 This playthrough comments on achievements in the game https://www.youtube.com/watch?v=hAhSaVsriZg

32 Achievements have been part of gaming since the 1980s as a way to reward gamers for completing all aspects of a game. Many gamers use them as a scorecard. There are divided opinions about their usefulness and often indie games do not include achievements. *Beyond Eyes* is the only game in the review in which Achievements will be noted as they are particularly apt in suggesting Rae's emotional response to her experience.

33 The "further away" truths are identified at https://www.xboxachievements.com/game/beyond-eyes/achievement/105416-truth.html

34 Short walkthrough at IndieDirect, https://www.youtube.com/watch?v=r79WCE_wKbM. Full walk through at https://www.youtube.com/watch?v=Sdhs2HfThVQ

35 https://www.edinventa.com/en-GB/heromask-languages-mathematics/, https://www.jetlearn.com/blog/virtual-reality-headset-kids, https://www.bobcooney.com/is-vr-safe-for-kids/

36 Vision Fountain's VR cultural experiences are aimed at those over 10. Read their take on the technology and testing done to date at https://www.visionfountain.com/2022/08/01/assessing-the-impact-of-vr-virtual-reality-headsets-on-under-13-year-olds/

37 See Richard Lico's test at https://vimeo.com/228262502

38 See Accessibility Reviews at https://caniplaythat.com/2019/01/29/deaf-game-review-moss/review and video posted on Facebook in American Sign Language at https://www.facebook.com/watch/?v=464470617299523

39 Playthrough at https://www.youtube.com/watch?v=LmiKBPnQ61E, play at https://www.myabandonware.com/game/hunchback-2h8

40 *Peter Pan, The Adventure Game (1984), Hook (1992), Peter Pan, A Story Painting Adventure (1993), Peter Pan, Adventures in Neverland (2002).*

41 Written at the beginning of the 20th century when sentiments differed, this comic approach to disability was common. Similar theatrical and film presentations influenced generations throughout the 1900s.

42 Although this is never addressed directly in the film, there has always been an assumption by fans that a tiny crack visible on the egg that would be him was the cause of Nemo's shorter fin.

43 https://movie-sounds.org/disney-movie-sound-clips/quotes-with-sound-clips-from-finding-nemo/he-was-born-with-it-kids-we-call-it-his-lucky-fin

44 The evolution of *Finding Nemo* games based on the film: *Finding Nemo* (GBA), *Finding Nemo* (PS2, Gamecube, XBOX), *Finding Nemo* (PC), *Nemo's Underwater World of Fun* (PC), *Finding Nemo 2* (GBA), *Finding Nemo: Escape to the Big Blue* (DS, 3DS), *Nemo's Reef* (iOS, Android), *Disneyland Adventures* (X360, PC, XB1, *Rush a Disney Pixar Adventure* (X360, PC, XB1), *Disney Infinity 3.0* (PS4, XB1, PS3), *Finding Dory* (Android, iOS), https://www.youtube.com/watch?v=hQ5dlupP_Xo. The most recent iteration is now available on steam as *Disney-Pixar Finding Nemo* and has two storylines taken from the film at https://store.steampowered.com/app/331450/DisneyPixar_Finding_Nemo/

Works Cited

Cainelli, E. A. (2022, December 24). Neurodevelomental disorders. Past, present, and future. *Children (Basel)*, *10*(1), 31.

Currys PC World. (2019). *Mental health and disabilities* (C. P. World, Producer). Retrieved from Diversity in Gaming: https://techtalk.currys.co.uk/tv-gaming/gaming/diversity-in-gaming/games-and-disabilities.html

Henderson, M. S. (1997). *Star Wars: The magic of myth.* New York, NY: Bantam Spectra.

Sullivan, P. (2015, November 1). *Pulse review – A great idea blinded by poor mechanics.* Retrieved from Cog Connected: https://cogconnected.com/review/pulse-review-a-great-idea-blinded-by-poor-mechanics/

5 The Games II, Neurodevelopmental Disability

Introduction

This chapter continues the discussion of games begun in Chapter 4 and moves on from representation of physical disabilities to that of neurodevelopmental disabilities.

Here are some facts worth repeating from previous chapters. WHO research shows that 16% of the world population or 1.6 billion people live with a disability. A 2020 study of over 3,000 players 16–50 in the UK and the US showed 29% and 31%, respectively, who self-identified as having a disability, with mental health being most reported. Interest over the past decade has resulted in those in the gaming industry taking some steps forward in use of representation. Currys PC World study on Diversity in Gaming (2019) reported that in the games they reviewed, 54% showed physical disability and the remainder either mental, sensory, mental/physical, or sensory/physical.[1]

Industry studies and articles are of teen and adult games, but the trend of more representation is also visible in our study's lists of PEGI 3 and PEGI 7 games. Studies and discussions concerning representation in children's media, however, are still predominantly about television.[2] These include the 2017 article about Julia in *Sesame Street Muppets* who has autism, the 2019 study *Is TV Making Your Child Prejudiced?*, and the 2021 Nora Inclusive Classroom Project suggestions for parents for inclusive programmes *Representation Station: Children's TV Shows*.

Fandom, the largest game fan wiki site, now includes a Diversegaminglists Wiki which has lists of Characters with Autism in Video Games, Games about Anxiety, Games about Depression, and Games about Psychosis.[3] The introduction to Chapter 4 stated that "children's games which represent disability authentically are often developed by individuals with family, friends, or colleagues who have the disability, or organizations who advocate for inclusion and understanding." This is particularly the case for disabilities which are neurodevelopmental. In the past, the quality of games has often suffered because of lack of funds for professional production; more recently games that are experimental or take on difficult disabilities to represent have had

DOI: 10.4324/9781003430445-5

a better chance of being made, and being made well, because of funding available through crowdsourcing and an increased interest in diversity and inclusion. But let's put this in perspective. The popular adult game, *Spec Ops: The Line* (2012, M17+), loosely based on Joseph Conrad's *Heart of Darkness*,[4] and which includes the character Captain Konrad who has psychosis ("You must think that I'm a monster…that I've gone insane. I came to terms with what I am a long time ago.")[5] sold 1.2 million hard copies in 2013, its first year of release, and 3.6 million copies so far on Steam, and has a gross revenue of $67.3 million.[6] In comparison, the indie game, *Max, an Autistic Journey*, has a revenue estimate of $5,000 since its release on Steam in 2016.[7] In a new social media world, such games do have the opportunity to be exposed to much bigger audiences then was once possible. It is, however, still very advantageous for those working towards inclusion to have authentically represented characters in popular games that reach a larger market, such as Lennie in *Geoffrey Goes to the Fair* in 1998, Winnie the Pooh and his friends throughout the years, and Dory in *Finding Nemo* more recently.

Memory Loss

Finding Nemo; Finding Dory: Just Keep Swimming

As discussed at the end of the previous chapter, characters with disabilities that children are familiar with from books, television shows, and movies are also often featured in video games. Children's previous exposure to these characters has created a schema which they bring forward into their play with the games. What adults may see as a disability will not have the same stigma with children. Marlin says Nemo's shorter fin is his Lucky Fin, an adult take on the disorder. But Nemo comfortably and competently swims everywhere the other fish do, and for him, and his viewing children's audience, his short fin is just that, a short fin, not a disability.[8]

As they do with Nemo, children bring the schema they've created of the way Dory remembers things from the movie into game play. Dory has a memory impairment or disorder and does not embed short-term memory. Dory doesn't retain what she's just heard, finds it difficult to recall who she just met, and can't remember where she's supposed to be going; at times those around her can get annoyed because she repeats herself a lot. The representation of her disability is accurate (Baxendale, 2004; Brinckman, 2013; Porter, 2020). Dory remembers better when she is around familiar things and people. When travelling with Marlin, she can repeat the address in Sydney and when Marlin is about to give up looking for Nemo she asks him not to, "I just, I remember things better with you" (Taylor, 1989). The movie shows her as a character who is curious, positive, and always trying to help others.

Her forgetfulness throughout the film creates some difficult situations and she is often apologetic; as she is ultimately successful in her endeavours because she tries and tries again, her apologizing is less obsequiousness than it is an indication of her social mores and desire to fulfil what she sees as her obligations.[9]

Dory is one of the three playable characters in the side-scrolling action game *Finding Nemo*, released in 2003. The game is rated E and PEGI 3. Dory is featured in the Mask Search in which she and Nemo dive into the abyss to retrieve P. Sherman's mask, which Dory has accidently dropped. The cut scenes between each challenge have her acting forgetfully when she meets someone and playing out the Dory trope "You look just like the fish back there." Nemo's father reacts to her forgetfulness with exasperation, Dory's positive response always negates this. There is no disadvantage to playing Dory, her ability to manoeuvre is the same as the others. In the schema of disability being created by Dory and her memory disorder, her persistence and cheerfulness become attributes of someone with such a disorder. The representation of her disability is authentic, although, as with most animation characters like Dory, the positive and cheerful attributes her character has may not be totally realistic.

Dory got her own side-scrolling game in *Finding Dory: Just Keep Swimming*, an online app released in 2016 and made to promote the film of the same name.[10] The game was rated 5+ by Common Sense Media in the US; there was no PEGI rating. Dory begins the movie and the game by stating outright that she suffers from short-term memory loss and immediately displays forgetting something. In the game, she is determined to tell the story of finding her parents, Charlie and Jennie, despite the faulty memory and does so via the cut scenes between games. Dory's long-term memory is triggered by things that happen to her in the present and prompt a flashback. She grows more confident with remembering. Representation is of a positive approach, lack of self-consciousness, persistence, and a confident "I knew I'd find you!" at the end. Unfortunately, as with the *Finding Nemo* video game, it is a traditional puzzle and action game and has no reference to activities related to memory loss. Practice at being skilled to gain mastery of the actions could cause frustration with the 11 levels of play and different types of puzzles to solve, bubbles to pop, and eels to avoid. Game play supports the players success: when Dory falls behind because the player wasn't quick enough in directing her or bumped into too many walls, the game mechanics help: Dory retells that part of the story so it can be played again. As a simple side-scroller with cut scenes, this game reiterates the story in the film but allows children to be successful in interacting with Dory to provide a positive representation of accomplishment for a character with a disability. As the game shows Dory's personality only in cut scenes and the activities have nothing to do with her memory loss, it is less authentic in its representation than is the movie.

Depression, Anxiety, and the "Bear of Little Brain"

Winnie the Pooh in the Hundred Acre Wood

Winnie the Pooh and his friends, Eeyore and Piglet, are iconic story characters created by A.A. Milne in 1926. Walt Disney licensed film (and other) rights in 1961, released the film *Winnie the Pooh and the Honey Tree* in 1966, and defined the characters in new ways.[11] Five more shorts and movies were released before the first game *Winnie the Pooh in the Hundred Acre Wood* was released in 1985. The game is a single player text adventure with 2D graphics and a text dialogue box which contains a description of the scene and simple instructions to go east, west, north, and south (in the dos version).

Each of Pooh's friends has a distinct personality. Incidents of Eeyore's depression and Piglet's anxiety commonly appear in stories, and their friends, especially Pooh with his very little brain, help to get them through situations that are distressing to them.[12] Eeyore is regularly seen with his head hanging, making comments about how difficult life is, and getting progressively more gloomy throughout the day. This and other ways he acts are accurate portrayals of a depression disorder. Piglet is constantly flustered and anxious about events, thinking that they will go wrong. He shakes and is often scared or nervous. His behaviour is an accurate portrayal of an anxiety disorder (Caves, 2019; Shea, 2000). Over time, Eeyore has become a symbol of depression and Piglet of anxiety. In this early game, the image of Piglet shows him pink and smiling, with no anxiety. The image of Eeyore shows him with his head hanging down and displays the text "Eeyore is standing by his house of sticks, thinking gloomy thoughts." The perception children have of the representation of disability is a function of the familiarity they have had with the characters prior to this game experience, as there is minimal action in the game which will encourage a different perception. Piglet is often seen doing happy things as his anxiety is not all-pervading but situation-based. Eeyore is always gloomy, and the descriptive text and his hanging head confirm children's past experience, reinforcing the existing schema they have of Eeyore. It is likely that young children do not yet have as part of their vocabulary the words anxiety or depression. They would instead have a sense of what Piglet and Eeyore feel like and are sympathetic towards them.

Winnie the Pooh: Preschool

Children can interact with Piglet at his most anxious in the game *Winnie the Pooh: Preschool* (1999). This is an educational game intended for the youngest in PEGI 3 that consists of typical preschool activities in a Hundred Acre Wood setting: counting carrots in Kanga's garden, learning French words at Pooh's echo tree, or painting a picture at Piglet's house. Winnie the Pooh is intent on giving Eeyore a birthday party and Piglet gets increasingly anxious because of the party planning and not having something to give Eeyore. Indicative of his supportive nature, Pooh paints a picture that Piglet can give to Eeyore as a present. There is some mastery of game mechanics required but the games are very simple and designed for young children, so frustration, except for the youngest and most inexperienced players, is minimal. As with all anthropomorphic creations, Winnie the Pooh and friends are real for young children and the feelings they have of sympathy are also real. At the party, Eeyore is a little embarrassed to let everyone know that it is not his birthday. This is Eeyore's character. Winnie the Pooh, who calls himself the bear of little brain, says it is his fault, he got it wrong. And then suggests that, as they are all there, they should make the best of it by having just a party. This exposition and recognition of an unapparent intellectual disability is a positive reflection of self-awareness without embarrassment. It is done within the cultural more of supporting a friend and this event adds to his schema. Pooh's comment is incidental to continuing the party, as for a moment it looked like they'd have to close it down. The representation of Piglet's anxiety is shown through the cut scenes interspersed between the games. Even though only seen for a few moments, the anxiety is recognizable. It is incidental to Pooh painting the picture. As with Dory's memory loss, Piglet's anxiety is improved by tasks being completed and friends being close, as in the party scene, where, picture delivered, he appears calm and happy. This is authentic representation that fills out the schema of Piglet.

Anxiety

Fractured Minds

In 2019, the single player adventure puzzle game, *Fractured Minds*, won the BAFTA Young Game Designers Award. Designed by Emily Mitchell, who has severe anxiety, the game is a puzzle adventure because "a puzzle is a good reflection of how mental health is in real life. It's a struggle to open the door into the next room" (Mitchell, 2019). The game is rated E, and PEGI 7 with the added descriptor Fear. The player navigates a series of six spaces titled chapters, some indoor, some outdoor, and the voyage into each chapter is prompted by a word that foreshadows the ambience of the space and the encounter with a characteristic of anxiety: Mundane, Emptiness, Comfort Zone, Paranoia, Sinking, and Monster. The interactivity is designed to elicit such feelings as fear, depression, a constant negative thinking that does not let up, and swing changes of mood which are associated with the different characteristics. The puzzles are deceptively simple but end up being emotionally difficult to complete as dread and a sense of failure permeate – in one room the word "wrong" repeats over and over and remains on screen as the player attempts to locate a correct key. There is a learning curve for each space as the player must figure out the puzzle and then solve it. Rather than skill, patience is called for as the player must repeat what are simple actions while being frustrated by waiting, as in for instance the need to wait to access drawers and cupboards until a red light passes. The need to wait patiently makes the game more suitable for middle years children as they move to pre-teen age rather than those at the younger end of PEGI 7. Middle years children also have more skills gained from their previous game play so that the different interactivity required for each room will not be as frustrating as it would be for younger children. That each room is a short, different puzzle will also be of interest to this age group who enjoy solving puzzles. If children play the game with the prompt that this is a simulation of anxiety, they will be able to build a schema of anxiety which includes the emotions the different puzzles elicit. Engaging with the different characteristics emotionally can encourage empathy, and with it compassion, and reduce the stigma associated with mental health issues that is often the cultural norm. Response to the game from those suffering anxiety indicates that these are actual characteristics, and that the simulation has a sense of reality[13] which makes the representation authentic.

Autism Spectrum Disorder, ADHD

Zanny, Born to Run

Zanny, Born to Run, released for IOS in 2010, and now unfortunately retired, is a funny, interactive story about a young boy who is on the autism spectrum[14] and cannot sit still.[15] Played on a tablet (or phone) this is an interactive picture book with pages that turn, text in the top left of the left-hand page, and full-page or full-spread illustrations of different places Zanny is familiar with, such as inside his house or outdoors on the grass. The main illustration on each page is static but objects on the page can be manipulated in different ways and Zanny can be made to zoom on the page. The story is told in a fun rhyme which reflects Zanny's busyness, and is illustrated with objects the player can move – the tablet can be tilted back and forth to make cheerios fall down or move up a page, or to make a shoe swing back and forth. Objects can be touched to make things happen – a flashlight can be turned on, and a robot doll's arms and legs made to move as Zanny is sleeping. The images portray the feeling that Zanny cannot sit still and needs to continuously run, even when he's sleeping.

The movables are simple to manipulate so that even the youngest child does not have difficulty in making amusing things happen on the page to create an engaging activity. The text connects the actions to Zanny's busyness, and the story needs someone who can read to make this connection. The interactive book is designed to show children 3+ who can't sit still that they are not alone in the world.[16] However, children aged 3–5 are generally not able to read and as they only interact with the movables, the activity does not translate into knowledge of the disability portrayed but simply provides the same type of fun as do many interactive storybooks. As a parent-child activity for children 3+, the story can provide an opportunity for discussion about Zanny as he is made to zoom across the pages by a little hand. It can introduce a positive and fun view of busyness to a child who may be as frustratingly busy as is Zanny. For children who already read, the text guides the interactivity with the purpose of sharing feelings about being busy kids; while they may find the activities simple, the interactivity encourages a connection with Zanny's emotions. The representation is incidental, Zanny's zooming starts the story, and instrumental, his busyness encourages active engagement in each page's activities. Written by an autistic child's parent, the situation it presents is authentic.

Axel's Chain Reaction

The ebook, *Axel's Chain Reaction,*[17] was awarded First Place for the Best Educational Digital Content for the Classroom in the US in 2015. The story is intended for children 6–9 and straddles PEGI 3 and 7. It introduces Axel, a grade 3 student who is a great tinkerer at home but is not doing so well at school. The interactive book shows that Axel is restless, inattentive, and finds it difficult to connect with classmates. These are characteristics of Autism Spectrum Disorder and Attention Deficit Hyperactivity Disorder (ADHD). At home, life is positive with Axel shown creating a domino chain reaction he shares with his mom. The first scenes in school are less positive; they include a basketball session that is very noisy and frustrating for Axel and a classroom scene in which he is daydreaming. His frustration and boredom changes to interest as the teacher shows three kinetic artist's work, including that of Alexander Calder, and asks the students to bring in recycled material and compete in making something from the materials. Like Alex, Calder also started making things when he was a boy. The rest of the story includes some creative problem solving in which players can participate through touch, tilt, tap, and shake actions that make things happen. There are a couple of failed attempts by Axel, with encouragement from his parents, both about the project itself (dad) and about how to handle the frustration of a failed attempt (mom). Players help him finish the sculpture and he brings it to school. In school on the final day, a bully pushes Alex and starts a disastrous chain reaction in which most of the student's projects are broken, amongst a lot of noise and confusion similar to that at the basketball game. Alex seems better able to handle the situation now and says he can help fix the projects. After some cooperation from everyone, the show proceeds. At the end everyone can take a picture of themselves, and if players are inspired, there are additional building projects to explore.

Representation of disability is incidental as Alex's neurodiversity is the basis of his tinkering and enthusiastic participation in the class challenge. It is also instrumental as his frustration at his failed attempts require his parents to work with him through a process of rebuilding confidence and composure.

His building attempts move him from stability to crisis as he is learning how to master his tinkering skills and his parents provide the tools and support he needs to help him through this period. This is an age at which collaboration skills are being developed, and the disaster creates a situation in which the abilities and skills Alex has developed because of his ADHD are acknowledged positively so that collaboration can happen. Axel is seen as a creative problem solver, no longer a problem. The representation of the disability as a difficulty at the start of the book is followed by successful completion of creative projects. This is similar to Kenny's story in *Backyard Baseball Junior* in which the introductory scenario shows his disability has some drawbacks, but this is followed with success. *Axel's Chain Reaction* provides a positive spin on representation of a disability by having players participate in the success that can occur when children with ADHD engage in activities suitable to their talents.

Max, an Autistic Journey

In *Max, an Autistic Journey* the player gets to spend the day with ten-year-old Max, who has been diagnosed with autism and ADHD. Released in 2016, this is an old style, 2D role-playing game with many mini-games and with pop-ups that provide information about autism and explain about autistic behaviour as Max displays it. Although there doesn't seem to be a rating available, it requires a fluent reader and would be more suitable for the upper end of PEGI 7. The player goes along with Max on his daily activities through his home and school, talking to his family and friends, playing mini-games to progress or to calm himself down, and battling a few monsters that represent his anxieties. The screen has an anxiety meter in the top right that goes up as Max goes through the day, the centre panel is the game space, and Max's face appears superimposed on this occasionally to show he's pleased, questioning, anxious, or very angry. The overt portrayal of emotion on his face prompts similar reaction by a player when this happens. Max needs to follow his daily routine strictly to keep his anxiety level low, and if it starts to rise, he can bring it down by controlling his breathing. If it hits the top, Max has a major tantrum that makes life difficult for everyone around him.

Max's behaviour displays autistic characteristics: as the noise increases in the classroom, his classmates start to look like monsters, he becomes anxious when he has to use a washroom he is not familiar with, he paints the same picture over and over again in art class, he tells a friend he's boring and can't figure out why he gets upset, he strikes out with immoderate actions when angry. The characteristics are described by information pop-up cards. The following one which appears in the homework scene is typical.

The meltdown... The anxiety attack... This is probably one of the most difficult facts of life with an ASD, both for the person with the ASD and for his loved ones... It's a loss of control, often seen as a completely disproportionate… An emotional flooding that takes over and stifles all easing… for a parent, it's a most challenging time. For a person with an ASD, it's hell… With Max, in order to not only stop the emotional floodings as they occur, but also try to prevent them, breathing and meditation are two tools with which we have had the most success. However, an important finding we made is this. Although the crisis is stopped, anger and anxiety will remain. Breathing is the first step to preventing (or stopping) a crisis. The second step is to let out aggression, stress, rage in a controlled and safe manner! We all must blow off steam!!

These information cards make the game an interesting mix of education and entertainment in an older style that would sit comfortably between the original *Carmen Sandiego* (1990) and *Dragon Quest V* (1992) games. It isn't necessary to access the information panels to play the game, as the dialogue and narrative in the text bar provide sufficient information to get to the next part of Max's Day. The dialogue with an adult is often didactic, if not preachy, as when the teacher talks about bullying. The game is more entertaining without the info panels but there are some nuggets which will help with playing the game, such as the information about the need to keep calm by doing breathing exercises. This information helps the player know about keeping Max's anxiety level down in the indicator so he doesn't explode. For children playing the game, learning such rules increases their mastery and helps with decision-making. Each mini-game is different from the others and has its own mechanics with some mini-games more complicated than others to complete. This can make the overall game more frustrating for children to play because there is never any certainty about what skill they will be required to use or improve on in the next mini-game; this may be intended to show that each new experience to an autistic person can create anxiety; if so, it succeeds.

The narrative situates itself in the contemporary world and makes itself more relevant by referencing popular culture: Sauron and the Mountain of Doom from Lord of the Rings (14+), Hans Solo from Star Wars (13+), Jon Snow from Game of Thrones (14+), and Five Night's at Freddy's (12+), all of which, although rated for older children, have probably been seen and/or played by pre-teens. The last two seem more adult references and the game, although it was intended to reflect a ten-year old's experience, presumably to other ten-year olds, does have a significant tinge of "game to inform adults about autism" sense about it. The contemporary references counter the old game aesthetics but this aesthetics does not lend itself to authenticity. So that while Max's emotions may be expressed by his superimposed face (happy or angry), the RPG game play with its 2D graphics and text interface do not lend themselves to the player experiencing Max as a person. Even though the game provides a "day in the life of Max," there seems little in the different scenes and their mini-games that creates a cohesive, informative, and interesting narrative about Max the complete person. The game defines him by his autism. It reinforces for children the schema that people who are autistic can only be defined by characteristics related to their autism not their humanity, and that other people do not share any of their characteristics. The narrative, from his parents being shocked by the doctor's diagnosis of autism, to the comment that his autism is a gift, fits into a social model of disability that representation stereotypically sustains and does not authentically provide children with a picture of Max, only of Max's autism. In that way, sadly, it is authentic.

Auti-Sim

Auti-Sim (2013) is an experimental prototype of a first-person game which causes the player the kind of irritation felt by someone who is autistic and has hypersensitivity. The game was inspired by a section in the documentary *Inside Autism* which shows the impact of a noisy classroom environment on a teenager.[18] The intent of the game was not to simulate hypersensitivity but "to elicit the same kind of reaction from a neurotypical person. So the goal was basically to irritate the hell out of your senses."[19] In the game, the player walks through a playground and as they come closer to groups of children playing, the noise and visual static increase until the environment is filled with audio and visual distortion that is almost unbearable. As the player moves in and out of the range of children playing, the noise and static also increase and reduce. Relief comes only as the player moves away from the other children completely and all is quiet again when the player is by themselves in a peaceful, treed area. Not rated, this game is best included in PEGI 7 because of the disturbing audio.

The playground environment entered in the game is one with which a middle years player would be familiar (at least one expects so). Children are playing on play equipment, running around, chatting. The way in which the player would normally participate in such an environment, walking or running up to friends to play, is one that they would have experienced themselves. The contrast between their usual experience and the noise and static in the game gives children an experience different from their normal one and shows what someone with autism might be feeling. Such exposure provides the type of information middle years children are interested in as they explore the boundaries of the world around them and can lead to comprehension that can change attitudes about, for instance, a new student with ADHD coming into their classroom.[20] Response to the game from individuals who experience hypersensitivity as part of their autism was that the simulation is accurate. Health and social workers commented that the responses of the child in the game compared to what they had seen in their work and how useful it was to better understand the characteristics of their clients.[21] Because of its authenticity, this representation may be effective in encouraging players to develop new attitudes towards the disorder.[22]

Dementia

Ether One

Another game which provides the experience of a neurobiological disorder is *Ether One*. Rated as PEGI 7, this first-person adventure puzzle game takes the player into the mind of Jean Thomson, a patient with dementia. The player engages first-hand with images from Jean's mind as "the Restorer," someone who enters the minds of patients and cures them of mental illnesses by repairing their broken memories. As details of Jean's life in the mining town of Pinwheel unfold, and her dementia progresses, her memories become increasingly disordered and chaotic, reflecting the deterioration of her cognitive abilities. The Restorer, as narrator, adds an external view and a comment that searching through memory is an experiment that may have been taken too far: the process of memory searching is questioned. This representation of concern about process is one middle years children would take up in their quest for understanding the world, asking if it is fair to invade Jean's mind. The progression of the story is separated from the many mind puzzles that a player can engage with throughout the game. Each puzzle reenforces a characteristic of dementia and adds to the player's experience of the disorder. The first-person play in the game is more experiential and personal than third person play and brings the reality of the confusion more authentically to the player. Because the representation is authentic, playing the game provides a seriousness and weight to the depiction that influences the schema being created and ultimately the perception children have of dementia. For children who may have a family member with dementia, the game can help with understanding a disorder that is difficult to comprehend.

Most of the games discussed in this and the previous chapters have been rated by PEGI, by the ESRB, and possibly by independent parent groups. The next chapter provides a short history of the rating systems conferred on the games, and some examples of the difficulty of getting it right.

Notes

1 https://techtalk.currys.co.uk/tv-gaming/gaming/diversity-in-gaming/games-and-disabilities.html
2 Discussions about influence of video games on children have proliferated for over 40 years. This has resulted in a large body of literature which unfortunately has not included much on representation of disability.
3 https://diversegaminglists.fandom.com/wiki/Category:Disability_and_Disorders
4 https://www.vgfacts.com/game/specopstheline/
5 https://specops.fandom.com/wiki/John_Konrad
6 https://vginsights.com/game/50300
7 https://games-stats.com/steam/game/max-an-autistic-journey/
8 Recall here the discussion about disorder or impairment and disability – the disorder being the actual physical issue, and the disability being how society treats that disorder (WHO, 2013).

9 There are varying opinions about this. Canadians are noted for using the phrase "I'm sorry," as a constant in their conversations. As such, apologizing is a politeness and a cultural norm in Canada and this approach to life reflects in my interpretation of Dory.

10 The game was removed from the App Store in 2017 and is now available on Amazon Kids+, a paid subscription service for children. A Dory play set was also available for Disney Infinity until Avalanche software shut down in 2016.

11 This was received with much negative commentary from traditionalists who felt the integrity of the original story and illustrations was ruined through misuse. Disneyfication was added to the vocabulary as a term of derision.

12 Although Pooh's constant concern with his weight and Tigger's irrepressible bounciness have been noted as possible issues, they are not included as disabilities here.

13 Reviews at https://www.criticalhit.net/review/fractured-minds-review-a-concentrated-clever-exploration-of-life-with-mental-illness/ and https://thenerdstash.com/fractured-minds-review-someone-elses-shoes/

14 Neurodevelopmental disabilities such as Autism, Aspergers, and Attention Deficit Hyperactivity Disorder (ADHD) are developmental disorders that are neurological in origin. Depending on the disorder and its progression or severity, it can cause different social, communication, and behavioural challenges. Autism and Aspergers have recently been grouped under the umbrella ASD or Autism Spectrum Disorder. Autism and ADHD are sometimes found together.

15 There is still a playthrough available at https://vimeo.com/19110327. It is unfortunate that the app is no longer available. Had it been a book, it would still be in the library, had it been a CD-ROM or game cartridge, it would still be on the shelf to find and play (who doesn't keep their old consoles?). As an online item, someone needs to actively put it on a platform like Steam or Abandonware to make it available. In 2011, the developer also released *Little Lillie's Touch Book* about a little girl who has adverse reactions to touch which has been discontinued. Playthrough at https://www.youtube.com/watch?v=ueC2iuhw7e0

16 The game's author has two autistic children and was active in the autistic community, creating the group Extra Special Kids, communicating through FB and Twitter, and participating in creating and promoting ways, such as *Zanny, Born to Run*, to have children feel included. Date on social media apps indicates they were active during the year the app was released https://www.facebook.com/ExtraSpecialKids, https://twitter.com/ExtraSpecialApp.

17 Official trailer at https://www.youtube.com/watch?v=CBRTTYYCbII. The app was created by Columbian developer Higuera and won more than 20 awards, including the Golden Lamp Award (2015) and the Parent's Choice Award (2014). https://higuerastudios.com/en/portfolio/axels-chain-reaction-ebook

18 https://www.youtube.com/watch?v=sbNGy2NtsOA

19 https://arstechnica.com/gaming/2013/03/auti-sim-lets-you-experience-the-horror-of-sensory-overload/

20 Middle years children, as they move towards being pre-teens, often become passionate advocates for what they see as important causes. Greta Thunberg, who has Asperger's, began her interest in climate change at 8 and by 15 was known for her activism around the world (Watts, 2019).

21 https://arstechnica.com/gaming/2013/03/auti-sim-lets-you-experience-the-horror-of-sensory-overload/

22 A study that looked at effectiveness of the game in changing perceptions indicated, "Engagement with the virtual simulation resulted in heightened perspective taking, which subsequently increased emotional concern, helping intentions, and willingness to volunteer compared with the observation only or text vignette intervention" (Sarge, Kim, & Velez, 2020).

Works Cited

Baxendale, S. (2004, December 18). Memories aren't made of this: Amnesia at the movies. *BMJ, 329*(7480), 1480–1483.

Brinckman, D. (2013, April 18). *Just keep swimming: Aquatic advice for coping with amnesia.* Retrieved from NeuroPsyFi, The Brain Science Behind the Movies: https://www.neuropsyfi.com/reviews/finding-nemo

Caves, C. a.-R. (2019). *How contemporary Disney film can be used for mental health teaching in schools: A case study of Winnie the Pooh (2011) and Inside Out (2015).* Retrieved from RC Psych: https://www.rcpsych.ac.uk/docs/default-source/members/divisions/london/london-essay-prizes/london-charlotte-caves-med-essay-prize-november-2020.pdf

Mitchell, E. (2019). *Fractured minds.* Retrieved from Steam: https://store.steampowered.com/app/688740/Fractured_Minds/

Porter, B. (2020). *Finding Dory's memories: The neuroscience behind Disney Pixar's Finding Dory.* Retrieved from Dr. Blake Porter: https://www.blakeporterneuro.com/finding-dorys-memories-the-neuroscience-behind-disney-pixars-finding-dory/

Shea, S. E. (2000, December 12). Pathology in the Hundred Acre Wood: A neurodevelopmental perspective on A.A. Milne. *CMAJ, 163*(12), 1557–1559.

Taylor, S. E. (1989). *Positive illusions: Creative self-deception and the healthy mind.* New York, NY: Basic Books.

Watts, J. (2019, March 11). *Greta Thunberg, schoolgirl climate change warrior: 'Some people can let things go. I can't'.* Retrieved from The Guardiian: https://www.theguardian.com/world/2019/mar/11/greta-thunberg-schoolgirl-climate-change-warrior-some-people-can-let-things-go-i-cant

WHO. (2013). *How to use the ICF: A practical manual for using the international classification of functioning, disability and health (ICF).* Geneva: World Health Organization.

6   Content Rating Systems

Introduction

Games used in the study were chosen within the PEGI 3 and PEGI 7 categories with content suitable for children as young as three in one case and as young as seven in the other. The review was conducted using both PEGI and ESRB, two predominant systems in the UK and North America which have developed over decades and stem from ratings for films and television.[1] Rating systems for games aim to provide parents with a reliable and easy-to-use tool to help them make game playing choices for their children. Since first established, video game rating systems have gained acceptance with parents who believe they reflect the content and age-appropriateness of games they are considering for purchase. Following is a short history of the rating systems conferred on games and some examples of the difficulty of getting it right.

PEGI and ESRB

The appropriateness of content in entertainment media has been a concern since films became widely distributed in theatres in the early 1900s. The British Board of Film Censors in the UK and the Motion Picture Producers and Distributors Association in the US set in motion guidelines to regulate content for films in keeping with morals of the day in 1912 and 1930, respectively. The UK created a rating system which by 1982 had specific ages in its ratings – U, PG, 15, 18, R18. In the US, an extensive production code (Hays Code) was replaced by a voluntary, self-regulatory system of ratings in 1968 intended to both stave off the spread of censorship boards and as a guide to parents. This rating system was modified to G, PG, PG13, R, and NC-17 (previously X) in 1996. Similar systems were put into place for television and then videos. Original concerns were the content of films being produced for adults. Then, with television coming into people's homes, concern for the age-appropriateness of programmes for children became prevalent.

Rating systems for video games were first created in the early 1990s. In the 1970s and 1980s the audience for games was perceived as being primarily

DOI: 10.4324/9781003430445-6

children. With the confluence in the early 1990s of an increase in the number of game consoles in homes and the number of violent fighting games released, concerns of the effect on children of depictions of explicit violence and sexual content in interactive video games escalated. In the UK, the Video Standards Council (VSC) was established to inform retailers about the 1984 Video Recording Act which required all games to carry a classification agreed on by the BBFC. In 1989 the European Leisure Software Publishers Association (ELSPA) was created to rate video games released in Britain.[2] This system was replaced by the Pan-European Game Information (PEGI) system in 2003 which has been administered by VSC since 2012.[3] Initial ELSBA ratings were 3–10, 11–14, 15–17, and 18+. These evolved to PEGI 3, 7, 12, 16, and 18. The rating is based on appropriateness of content for children, not skill level. The PEGI rating is currently used in 35 European countries. PEGI age ratings correlate to children's cognitive development as discussed in earlier chapters and are a useful guide for parents who are interested in the suitability of a game for their child's age.

PEGI Ratings as of 2023[4]

PEGI 3 – Suitable for all age groups. The game should not contain any sounds or images likely to scare young children. No bad language should be used.

PEGI 7 – Suitable for those aged 7 or above. There could be mild forms of violence, and some scenes might be frightening for children.

PEGI 12 – Suitable for those aged 12 or above. The game could feature more realistic and graphic scenes of violence.

PEGI 16 – Suitable for those aged 16 or above. This rating is used when the violence becomes realistic and would be expected in real life. Bad language and the use of tobacco, alcohol, or illegal drugs can also be present.

PEGI 18 – Suitable for those aged 18 or above. The adult classification is used when there are extreme levels of violence and motiveless killing. Glamorization of drugs, gambling, and sexual activity can also be featured.

PEGI! – For some non-game apps such as Facebook, Twitter, or YouTube. Serves as a warning that these apps can offer a broad variety of user-generated or curated content.

In the US, states could censor sales of games because of obscenity but not violence. As a result, during Congressional hearings in 1994, a video game rating act was introduced to regulate content and labelling.[5] The act was not passed and in an effort to self-regulate rather than be regulated, the Entertainment Software Association (ESA) put into place a rating system for video games to be directed by the Entertainment Software Review Board (ESRB).[6] Initially the ESRB created five age-based ratings and included younger children: Early Childhood (eC), Kids to Adults (K–A), Teen (T),

Mature (M), and Adults Only (AO). Kids to Adults was changed to Everyone in 1998.[7] E10+ was added in 2005 to differentiate between the entire family and children 10 and older. Descriptors, such as Comic Violence, were also added (2005) to identify for consumers the reason for the rating. There are now 30 or so descriptors which are used with the game ratings on the ESRB site, but as can be imagined, including them in game packaging or marketing, can be awkward. The Early Childhood (eC) rating was retired in 2018. An ESRB Twitter account comment made in April 2019 notes, "Yes, we retired the eC rating last year around this time. There were SO few games that fit the criteria, and the argument could almost always be made that E was also applicable for those titles!" The estimation "Few games" is contrary to the many titles produced for young children every year and belies the market which the almost 900 million downloads of *Toca Life* around the world reveals. Elimination of this age rating denies that children's needs and skills, as established by child development research, are different from those of older children, teens, and adults, and makes the current ESRB rating system, ostensibly originally created to protect children, inadequate and inferior to other rating systems.

ESRB Ratings as of 2023[8]

Everyone (E) – Games with this rating contain content that the ESRB believes is suitable for all ages, including minimal cartoon, fantasy or mild violence, and/or the infrequent use of mild language.

Everyone 10+ (E10+) – Games with this rating contain content that the ESRB believes is suitable for ages 10 and over, including cartoon, fantasy, or mild violence, mild language, and/or minimal suggestive themes.

Teen (T) – Games with this rating contain content that the ESRB believes is for ages 13 and over, including violence, suggestive themes, crude humour, minimal blood, and/or infrequent use of strong language.

Mature 17+ (M) – Games with this rating contain content that the ESRB believes is suitable for ages 17 and over, including intense violence, blood and gore, sexual content, strong language, drug use, nudity, and/or crude humour.

Adults Only 18+ (AO) – Games with this rating contain content that the ESRB believes is suitable for ages 18 and over, including prolonged scenes of intense violence and/or graphic sexual content.

The increasing global prevalence of video games motivated individual countries to evaluate existing rating systems and, in some cases, create their own, both because they were now creating their own games and because they had their own approaches to child development and what content might be appropriate for different age groups.[9]

Usefulness

Content rating systems can be opaque, leaving parents questioning how a rating was arrived at. Descriptors have been added to the PEGI and ESRB ratings to assist parents with both understanding why a game was included in a rating as well as to assist with making decisions about purchase. Parent-based advocacy consumer groups have stepped in to provide more information and fill in gaps through sites which provide reviews as well as articles relevant to gaming. Four sites are particularly useful for reference as they provide extensive databases on the content of games. In the UK, AskAboutGames[10] is a joint venture between the VSC Rating Board and games trade association UKIE (previously ELSPA). It has a database of 2452 games (2023) which it has tested with families and for which it provides reviews, including skill ratings. The site also helps with information on setting up gaming systems, keeping gaming costs down, setting ground rules, game events of interest to families, and covers socially relevant topics such as staying in touch with grandparents. UK-based TamingGaming.com[11] is a database for families which includes both PEGI and ESRB ratings as well as the following categories of games: Preschoolers 2–4, Little Kids 5–7, Big Kids 8–9, Tweens 10–12, Younger Teens 13–15, Older Teens 16+. The site provides a skill rating as well as reports on the accessibility features of games. It includes lists of games designed for reduced motor function, deaf and hard of hearing, autistic diversity, reduced fine motor control, without sight, and other points of accessibility that make it possible to find games for players with different kinds of disabilities. Lists under Mental Health include "Walk in Someone Else's Shoes" and "Space for Loneliness." Under Accessibility is found "Designed for Players without Sight."[12] Included in this last list are games such as, *A Blind Legend* in which the player plays a blind knight, and *Blind Drive*, an audio game in which the player is blindfolded, handcuffed to a car, and drives against the traffic. These are for teens or adults, not children.

One of the most popular rating sites in the US is Common Sense Media (CSM)[13] which provides three kinds of ratings, one by an expert panel, one based in parent's reviews, and another based in kid's reviews. It uses narrow age ranges: 0–2, 3, 4, 5, 6, 7, etc., but also categorize more broadly 2–4, 5–7, etc., as per TamingGaming in the previous paragraph. The site has a secondary five-star rating for Educational Value, Positive Messages, Positive Role Models and Representations, Ease of Play, Violence, Sex, Language (Bad), Consumerism, Drinking, and Drugs and Smoking (note the other sites mentioned have this second level as well, each with their own set of descriptors). It also has an extensive base of information for parents about games and their use as both entertainment and education, including articles on the need for diversity in games. It has recently added "diverse representations" in its list of considerations (gender mainly); accessibility is currently not addressed. A site which reviews games for gamers who love games and now have their own children with whom they would like to play, or whose games they'd like to monitor, is Pixelkin.[14] The site is not as extensive as CSM's but does include information such as how games are used in schools. As a plus for those who like a preview of the game, it often includes trailers.

Difficulties

There are three main difficulties with age ratings. One, they are based in cultural norms which means a game can have different ratings depending on who reviewed it and for what site. This is one reason countries such as Australia and Germany have chosen to use their own system. PEGI and ESRB are based in different cultural norms, as are the different consumer rating systems which have sprung up, and which the ratings and the descriptors confirm. The game *Overcooked!* is rated PEGI 3 for 3–6, E for Everyone, and 8+ by CSM. The game *Last Day of June* is rated PEGI 7 for 7–12, E for everyone, and 10+ by CSM. The game *Ether One* is rated PEGI 7 with the descriptor Fear, and E10+ with descriptors Alcohol and Tobacco Reference, Mild Language, Mild Violence (no CSM rating yet). Adults considering these games can feel justifiably confused about which age the games were suitable for.

Two, accurately accessing the age group for which the content of a game is most suitable is difficult. For some games this is obvious, for others unclear or ambiguous. Each child is an individual and has capacities, abilities, and experiences different from that of the child sitting next to them playing the same game. Which, of course, is one reason there is an age "range". Even given this range, some children of 7 and 8 have played and are comfortable with complex, emotionally driven games so that that representation of mental health issues such as in *Ether One* will cause them little fear and frustration. Others, who are less experienced emotionally, may feel a greater sense of dread even at age 10 or 12 at the increasing level of confusion in the images and actions of the dementia patient, Jean.

Three, skill level may not correlate to the age category and frustrate children, making for more and more intense crisis periods when they are given a game which, purportedly, they should be able to play. Children of the same age have different capabilities and abilities whether they are working to achieve mastery of a skill or to collaborate with another player. Fortunately, increased awareness of this difficulty has meant that a number of review sites provide a skill rating to inform a parent about how easily playable a game is for a certain age. Examples of how ratings may not accurately show suitability for an age group are two games similar in their gameplay, *Overcooked!* and *Moving Out*.

Overcooked! ratings are PEGI 3, ESRB Everyone, CSM 8+ with 4 out of 5 for Ease of Play, TamingGaming skill rating 7–13.
Moving Out ratings are PEGI 3. ESRB Everyone. CSM 8+ with 4 out of 5 for Ease of Play, TamingGaming skill rating 6+.

The *Overcooked!* online reviews say it is a fun, very fast-paced game that speeds up very quickly, and is stressful even at lower levels. *Moving Out* is noted at also speeding up but is never as fast or as stressful.[15] An analysis of the two games identifies several reasons why *Moving Out* is not as fast or stressful: the busyness of the activities (number of actions that are necessary to accomplish the task), the familiarity with the objects and activities, and the familiarity with the process. A cooking environment, which requires many small items to be acquired and moved quickly, is inherently busier than that of moving a home which includes the manipulation of a variety of different sized, some quite large, objects. Choosing ingredients, preparing them by chopping, then assembling them onto a plate, is a complex schema. While 3- to 5-year-olds may pretend to play in their toy kitchens, the purpose of their play is not speed. In *Overcooked!* the purpose is not pretend cooking, but speed. Young children (PEGI 3) are seldom able to undertake such an activity either cognitively or physically. By the time children are seven, i.e. beginning their middle years, most children have been exposed to demands of speed through kindergarten and early grade training and competitions and through playing games, and are more ready cognitively and physically to take on the challenge of *Overcooked!* without less frustration and failure. On the other hand, even children who are three years old are familiar with the objects in a home such as a lamp, rug, or sofa, and smaller items like paper, boxes, and especially toys, and have experienced moving these (maybe not the sofa). Cognitively they are prepared for such an activity. Physically, fine motor skills require refinement of mouse and controller click, point, and drag skills will increase with practice. Because *Moving Out* is occupied with both creating a narrative through pretend play, and how quickly that narrative can be completed, speed is mitigated. Both games, in particular *Overcooked!*, speed up and move players to a higher level of complexity quickly. There is an assumption that lower levels (fewer choices, slower play) deal with the needs of younger children, who should then be able to play these levels comfortably. This is not the case. Younger children may simply not have the cognitive and physical ability to take on the different tasks required and can become overly frustrated in their attempts to master these tasks which results in a more intense critical period in the form of tantrums. TamingGaming suggests 7–13 as the skill rating for *Overcooked!* which confuses the PEGI 3 rating for content.

Ratings are also unclear when looking at cooperative play, a feature of both *Overcooked!* and *Moving Out* which is reviewed as adding "more fun." Each child's ability to play cooperatively is based in their experience of such play and is a skill children begin to develop as they move from a dependent home environment to a more autonomous and social school environment, usually beginning ages 5–7. Even the less frantic cooperative play in *Moving Out* may be out of reach for those who have not had the opportunity to play with others this way. Cooperative play skills are more developed as children enter their middle years, age 7 or 8.

Are the ratings above any use to someone who is looking for guidance in purchasing these games? The skill ratings provided in TamingGaming map closest to the cognitive and physical capabilities of children shown through child development theory. Using the PEGI 3 or Everyone rating as a guide to purchasing these games for a child aged 3 is likely to result in the game being frustrating, if attractive. *Moving Out* will be easier to play than *Overcooked!* but only if a child of 5 is already a dedicated and proficient game player will they be able to keep up to speed without frustration.[16]

The PEGI system, with its breakdowns into different age groups, is more consistent with both child development theories and neurobiology than is the ESRB system with its large grouping of Everybody. More beneficial yet are the ratings and reviews provided by advice groups such as AskAboutGames, TamingGaming, Common Sense Media, and Pixelkin. AskAboutGames is particularly useful for sourcing games about disabilities.

Notes

1 Germany and Australia also have longstanding rating systems.
2 https://retrocdn.net/Entertainment_and_Leisure_Software_Publishers_Association
3 https://gamesratingauthority.org.uk/RatingBoard/about-history
4 https://en.wikipedia.org/wiki/PEGI
5 Congressional hearings, December 7, 1993, and March 5, 1994, cited the games *Mortal Combat, Night Trap,* and *Lethal Enforcer* as depicting realistic violence and affecting the psychological health of children and teens, as well as being addictive. See details at https://en.wikipedia.org/wiki/1993_United_States_Senate_hearings_on_video_games.
6 Germany's Entertainment Software Self-control (ESK) was also created in 1994.
7 "Video game ratings are great for today's games, but may struggle with gaming's future." Brian Crecente. Sep 22, 2014. https://www.polygon.com/2014/9/22/6828699/video-game-ratings-are-great-for-todays-games-but-may-struggle-with
8 https://en.wikipedia.org/wiki/Entertainment_Software_Rating_Board
9 A comparison graph shows individual countries' systems at https://en.wikipedia.org/wiki/Video_game_content_rating_system.
10 https://www.askaboutgames.com
11 AskAboutGames refers to the Taming Gaming database used when searching for a specific game. See at https://www.taminggaming.com
12 https://www.taminggaming.com/en-us/Designed+For+Players+Without+Sight
13 https://www.commonsensemedia.org
14 https://pixelkin.org
15 https://www.psu.com/news/hands-on-moving-out-is-house-removal-overcooked-without-the-stress/
16 Children's reviews of *Overcooked* suggest a range from 3+ to 6+. Children who provide reviews are often accomplished game players. See at https://www.commonsensemedia.org/game-reviews/overcooked/user-reviews/child

7 Final Words

Final Words

When Lennie took off downhill in his wheelchair to race Geoffrey and their friends on the way to the fair in 1998, he enjoyed a representation of his mobility impairment seldom found even today – authentic representation without bias or stigma. Positive representation of disability in games requires awareness and a shift in cultural perception, which is more difficult to achieve than innovation in technology. Two things help us in initiating the shift. Based on the premise that the perceptions we hold as adults are a result of not only our most recent experiences, but of experiences that go back to our formative years, it is useful to know how our perceptions are created and then maintained. With this information in hand, we can look at existing representation of disability and consider how, as children engage with a game and interact with its representation of disability, they integrate information about the disability. This gives us a way forward to designing games with better representation.

Chapter 1 notes that "With the emergence of each new communication technology used to provide information, education, or entertainment there have been groups of people who have been excluded from using that media because differing capabilities made it inaccessible to them." The World Health Organization has as a global goal that individuals of all capabilities can participate equally in our society. To achieve this goal, the current social model which sees impairment as a disability and people with an impairment stereotypically as suffering and needing a cure, requires a change in perception. With the prevalence of mobile technologies such as tablets and the increase in online availability and use of games for both education and entertainment for children, this engaging and interactive form of telling our stories is well placed to provide authentic representations of disability and initiate schema that are not based on stereotypes.

Games can best represent disability by avoiding stereotyping, adding accurate depictions, and constructing authentic meaning for the player. Existing games differ greatly in being able to achieve this goal because developers'

DOI: 10.4324/9781003430445-7

interests range from expanding market reach with a nod to diversity based on stereotypical views, to exploring impairments/disorders to reflect them accurately. In the analysis of games three broad categories prove useful. Games are cosmetic and neutral and provide exposure but not gameplay utility as in the game *Moving Out*. They are incidental and used as a device that provides purpose for the narrative, as in *Last Day in June*, or they authentically represent the disability and show how the character copes with their disability, as in *Axel's Chain Reaction*. Nuances are inevitable, cosmetic representation can be very basic, but also visually inclusive when the player can, for instance, customize their wheelchair as in *Animal House Crossing, New Horizons*. Incidental representation often carries with it an instrumental component when there is both an inciting event and ongoing motivation because of the disability, as in *Beyond Eyes*. Authentic representation can include not only the factual aspects of the disability, but also how it may affect daily life, as in *Ether One*. Along with many nuances is the possibility of intersection between categories, games are often both incidental and authentic.

How representation is perceived by children depends in large part on where they are in the cognitive development process. Are they still in their magic dreamworld with pretend play that is all about Eeyore and Piglet? Are they beginning to socialize outside their home and family and thinking about including Kenny in their next baseball team? Are they questioning the world and figuring out how they fit in it when they are experiencing Jean's confused thoughts? Whichever stage of development they are proceeding through, the dynamic schema that helps structure their experience of the world assimilates and accommodates new information about the many kinds of physical disability and neurodevelopmental disability that games now show, deafness in *Weakless*, blindness in *Pulse*, autism in *Max, an Autistic Journey*. Each new exposure and engagement external to the cultural norms that may mould young children with stereotypical views of disability, nuances their schema and moves it farther away from those cultural norms, especially as children aim to be autonomous and no longer dependent on their parents' ideas as they progress through later childhood towards adolescence.

The representation in the games identified in this review first exposes children to the disability and identifies its existence, then it encourages them to engage with the disability through different types of game interactivity, and finally it reifies the experience through repeated play. While there are issues in how representation of disability is at times simply cosmetic, or is not accurate, or is linked to characters parents may find violent, or told in frightening stories, today, more so than at any other time, each attempt at representation has a social world of reviewers and critics to mitigate its value.

Last words from the front lines.

The late Mike Fahey, senior reporter at Kotaku for many years, commented about the addition of a cosmetic wheelchair to *Animal Crossing: New Horizons*,

> *There is a wheelchair in Animal Crossing: New Horizons. It's nothing fancy. It doesn't roll. The power wheelchair I use in real-life would crush it like a monster truck. But it is there, in the game, and it makes me very happy.*[1]

Jessica Sergeant, deaf human rights activist, noted in a video reviewing *Moss* that although Quill really only signs a few times, including a mouse protagonist who signs in American Sign Language is a breakthrough approach.[2]

In the first ever talk on representation at GDC 2019, Aderyn Thompson said "The feeling of seeing even a glimpse of who you are in a positive light is profound. … It's a nudge that you are not alone, and more importantly, that you are welcome."[3]

Notes

1 "I'm So Happy There's a Wheelchair in Animal Crossing: New Horizon" https://kotaku.com/i-m-so-happy-there-s-a-wheelchair-in-animal-crossing-n-1842492728

2 Moss Facebook review in sign language, https://www.facebook.com/watch/?v=464470617299523

3 GDC Showcase: "You Can Take an Arrow to the Knee and Still Be an Adventurer" at https://www.youtube.com/watch?v=Vb39BFs1UK0&t=1s

Addendum I Game List

PEGI 3 Games in Review Chapters

1 **HunchBack.** 1983. Spinal Disorder. Auditory impairment.
2 **Peter Pan, the Adventure Game.** 1984. Mobility impairment upper limb.
3 **Winnie the Pooh and the Hundred Acre Wood.** 1984. Depression. Anxiety.
4 **Backyard Baseball Junior.** 1997. Ages 5–10. Mobility impairment lower limbs.
5 **Geoffrey Goes to the Fair.** 1998. Ages 3–10. CD-ROM. Mobility impairment lower limbs.
6 **Peter Pan, A Story Painting Adventure.** 1993. Ages 6–10. Mobility impairment upper limb.
7 **Disney's Winnie the Pooh Preschool.** 1999. Ages 3–5. Depression. Anxiety.
8 **Finding Nemo.** 2003. PEGI 3 Everyone. CSM 5+. Mobility impairment upper limb, Memory impairment.
9 **DreamBox Learning Math.** 2008. Ages 5–9. Mobility impairment lower limbs.
10 **Buster Baxter: Lung Defender.** 2010. Ages 4–8. Asthma.
11 **Zanny, Born to Run.** 2011. Ages 3–6. ADHD.
12 **Axel's Chain Reaction.** 2013. Ages 6–9. Autism Spectrum Disorder.
13 **Finding Dory: Just Keep Swimming.** 2016. CSM 5+. Memory impairment.
14 **Toca Life Series: Farm (Hospital, Town +).** 2018. Age 3+. Mobility impairment lower limbs.
15 **Peg and Pog.** 2018. Age 3–5. CSM 3+. Mobility impairment lower limbs.
16 **Weakless.** 2019. PEGI 3. Everyone. Visual and auditory impairment.
17 **Moving Out.** 2020. PEGI 3. Everyone. CSM 8+ Skill 6+ Mobility impairment lower limbs.

PEGI 7 Games in Review Chapters

1 **Sly 2: Band of Thieves.** 2004. PEGI 3. E (Cartoon Violence). Mobility impairment lower limbs.
   Sly 3: Honor Among Thieves. 2005. PEGI 7. E10+ (Cartoon Violence, Comic Mischief).
2 **Lego Marvel Super Heroes.** 2013. PEGI 7. E10+ (Comic Mischief, Mild Violence). CSM 10+, 7+, 6+. Mobility impairment lower limbs.
3 **Auti-Sim.** 2013. No age category. Autism Spectrum Disorder.
4 **Ether One.** 2014. PEGI 7. Everyone. Dementia.
5 **Beyond Eyes.** 2015. PEGI 7. Visual impairment.
6 **Pulse.** 2015. PEGI 7. CSM 13+. Visual impairment.
7 **Overcooked!** 2016. PEGI 7. Everyone (Mild Cartoon Violence). CSM 8+, 6+, 5+ Skill 7–13. Mobility impairment lower limbs.
8 **Max, an Autistic Journey** 2016. Autism Spectrum Disorder.
9 **Last Day of June.** 2017. PEGI 7. E10+ (Mild Violence). Mobility impairment lower limbs.
10 **Moss.** VR Game. 2018. E10+ (Fantasy, Violence) Commonsense 12+, 12+, 8+. Hearing impairment.
11 **Fractured Minds.** 2019. Anxiety.
12 **Lego Star Wars, The Skywalker Saga.** 2022. PEGI 7, E10+ (Cartoon Violence, Comic Mischief). Mobility impairment upper limb.

All Games Reviewed

PEGI 3

1 **HunchBack.** 1983. Spinal Disorder. Auditory impairment.
2 **Peter Pan, the Adventure Game.** 1984. Mobility impairment upper limb.
3 **Winnie the Pooh and the Hundred Acre Wood.** 1984. Depression. Anxiety.
4 **Peter Pan and the Pirates.** 1991. Mobility impairment upper limb.
5 **Hook.** 1992. Mobility impairment upper limb.
6 **Peter Pan, A Story Painting Adventure.** 1993. Ages 3–7. Mobility impairment upper limb.
7 **Camp Frog Hollow.** 1996. Ages 7–11. Mobility impairment lower limbs.
8 **The Hunchback of Notre Dame Animated Story Book.** 1996. Ages 3–9. Spinal Disorder. Auditory impairment.
9 **Backyard Baseball Junior.** 1997. Ages 5–10. Mobility impairment lower limbs.
10 **Geoffrey Goes to the Fair.** 1998. Ages 3–10. CD-ROM. Mobility impairment lower limbs.
11 **Disney's Winnie the Pooh Preschool.** 1999. Ages 3–5. Depression. Anxiety.

12 **Return to Never Land.** 2002. PEGI 3+. Everyone. Mobility impairment upper limb.

13 **Finding Nemo.** 2003. PEGI 3 Everyone. CSM 5+. Mobility impairment upper limb, Memory impairment.

14 **Joe Rock and Friends: Book 3.** 2007. Ages 3–9. Different disability in each story game.

15 **DreamBox Learning Math.** 2008. Ages 5–9. Mobility impairment lower limbs.

16 **Disney's A Christmas Carol.** 2009. Everyone. Comic Violence. CS 8+. Mobility impairment lower limbs.

17 **Buster Baxter: Lung Defender.** 2010. Ages 4–8. Asthma.

18 **Zanny, Born to Run.** 2011. Ages 3–6. ADHD.

19 **Axel's Chain Reaction.** 2013. Ages 6–9. Autism Spectrum Disorder.

20 **Frozen: Freefall.** 2013. 4+. Fantasy impairment.

21 **Toca Life Series: Farm (Hospital, Town +).** 2018. Age 3+. Mobility impairment lower limbs.

22 **Finding Dory: Just Keep Swimming.** 2016. CSM 5+. Memory impairment.

23 **Finding Dory Toy Box: Dory's Quest to Remember What Her Quest Was.** 2016. Everyone. Memory Impairment.

24 **Peg and Pog.** 2018. Ages 3–5. CSM 3+. Mobility impairment lower limbs.

25 **Weakless.** 2019. PEGI 3. Everyone. Visual and auditory disability.

26 **Moving Out.** 2020. PEGI 3. Everyone. CSM 8+ Skill 6+ Mobility impairment lower limbs.

PEGI 7

1 **Sly 2: Band of Thieves.** 2004. PEGI 3. E (Cartoon Violence).
 Sly 3: Honor Among Thieves. 2005 PEGI 7. E10+ (Cartoon Violence, Comic Mischief).
 Sly Cooper: Thieves in Time. 2013. PEGI 7 E10+ (Alcohol Reference, Cartoon Violence, Comic Mischief, Use of Tobacco). Mobility impairment of the lower limbs. Visual impairment.

2 **Kingdom Hearts 3D: Dream Drop Distance.** La Cité des Cloches from The Hunchback of Notre Dame. 2012. PEGI 12. ESRB E10+. Spinal Disorder. Auditory impairment.

3 **Lego Marvel Super Heroes.** 2013. PEGI 7. E10+ (Comic Mischief, Mild Violence). CSM 10+, 7+, 6+. Mobility impairment lower limbs.

4 **Auti-Sim.** 2013. No age category. Autism Spectrum Disorder.

5 **Ether One.** 2014. PEGI 7. E. Dementia.

6 **Beyond Eyes.** 2015. PEGI 7. Visual impairment.

7 **Pulse.** 2015. PEGI 7. CSM 13+. Visual impairment.

8 **Overcooked!** 2016. PEGI 7. Everyone (Mild Cartoon Violence). CSM 8+, 6+, 5+ Skill 7–13. Mobility impairment lower limbs.

9 **Max, an Autistic Journey** 2016. E. Autism Spectrum Disorder.
10 **Last Day of June**. 2017. PEGI 7. E10+ (Mild Violence). Mobility disability lower limbs.
11 **Celeste.** 2018. PEGI 7. E10+. CSM 10+. Anxiety. Depression.
12 **Moss.** VR Game. 2018. E10+ (Fantasy, Violence) CSM 12+, 12+, 8+. Hearing impairment.
13 **Granny Prix Multi-Player.** 2018. Grade based. Mobility impairment of the lower limbs.
14 **Once Upon a Coma.** 2018. PEGI 3. Depression.
15 **Dragons: Dawn of New Riders.** 2019. PEGI 7, E10+ (Fantasy, Violence), CSM 10+, 10+. Mobility impairment lower limbs.
16 **Spyro Reignited Trilogy.** 2019. PEGI 7 E10+ (Cartoon Violence, Comic Mischief). CSM 8+, P6+, K7+ Attention Deficit disorder.
17 **Fractured Minds.** 2019. PEGI 7. E. Severe anxiety.
18 **Neversong.** 2020. PEGI 7, E10+, CSM 10+. Previously Once Upon a Coma. Depression.
19 **Lego Star Wars, The Skywalker Saga.** 2022. PEGI 7, E10+ (Cartoon Violence, Comic Mischief). Mobility impairment upper limb.

PEGI 12

The Simpsons, Tapped Out, Teen 2016 update. Features Stephen Hawking. ALS, Lou Gehrig's Disease

PEGI 18

SpecOps: The Line. 2012. PEGI 18 (**Violence**, Bad Language) M17+ (Blood and Gore, Intense Violence, Strong Language) CSM 18+. PTSD.

Board Games

1 **Removing Barriers.** 2008. Board Game. 8+ Lower limb mobility impairment.
2 **The Stroke Game.** Board Game. 8+. Neurodevelopmental disorders.

Other Games Mentioned

LOGO (1967)
Reader Rabbit (1984)
Clifford's Fun With Letters (1988)
Arthur's Math Adventures (1999)
Giggles Computer Funtime for Babies (2006)
Dora's Number Pyramid Adventure Game (2023)

Bibliography

Alberti, L. B. (1991). *On painting* (C. Grayson, Ed.). London: Penguin.

Antle, A. (2004). Supporting children's emotional expression and exploration in online environments. *IDC '04 Proceedings* (pp. 97–104). ACM Digital Library.

Antle, A. (2008). Child-based personas: Need, ability and experience. *Cognition, Technology & Work, 10*(2), 155–166.

Antle, A. N. (2019). EmotoTent: Reducing school violence through embodied empathy games. *Proceedings of the 18th ACM international conference on interaction design and children* (pp. 755–760). New York, NY: Association for Computing Machinery.

Bakhtin, M. (1982). *The dialogic imagination: Four essays*. (M. Holquist, Ed., & C. E. Holquist, Trans.) Austin, TX: University of Texas Press.

Banich, M. T. (2011). *Cognitive neuroscience* (3rd ed.). Wadsworth, OH: Cengage Learning.

Bartlett, F. C. (1932). *Remembering: An experimental and social study*. Cambridge, MA: Cambridge University Press.

Baxendale, S. (2004, December 18). Memories aren't made of this: Amnesia at the movies. *British Medical Journal, 329*(7480), 1480–1483.

Blanck, P. (2019). Why America is better off because of the Americans with Disabilities Act and the Individuals with Disabilities Education Act. *Touro Law Review, 35*(1), 605–618.

Blumberg, F. C. (2013, Spring). The impact of recreational video game play on children's and adolescents' cognition. *New Directions for Child and Adolescent Development* (139), 41–50.

Blumberg, F. C.-D. (2019, February 15). Digital games as a context for Children's cognitive development: Research recommendations and policy considerations. *Social Policy Report, 32*(1), 1–33.

Blunden, A. (2008, July). *Vygotsky's unfinished theory of child development*. Retrieved 2016, from Marxist Internet Archive: https://www.marxists.org/archive/vygotsky/works/comment/vygotsky-on-development.pdf

Bodrova, E., & Leong, D. J. (2015). Vygotskian and post-Vygotskian views on Children's play. *American Journal of Play, 7*(3), 371–388.

Bower, T. G. (1976, November). Repetitive processes in child development. *Scientific American, 235*(5), 38–47.

Bransford, J. D. (Ed.). (2000). *How people learn: Brain, mind, experience, and school*. Washington, DC: National Academy Press.

Brinckman, D. (2013, April 18). *Just keep swimming: Aquatic advice for coping with Amnesia*. Retrieved from NeuroPsyFi, The Brain Science Behind the Movies: https://www.neuropsyfi.com/reviews/finding-nemo

Bruer, J. T. (2002). *The myth of the first three years: A new understanding of early brain development and lifelong learning*. New York, NY: Free Press.

Bruner, J. (1960). *The process of education*. Cambridge, MA: Harvard University Press.

Bruner, J. (1991, Autumn). The narrative construction of reality. *Critical Inquiry, 18*(1), 1–21.

Cahill, S. E. (1995, Autumn). Reconsidering the stigma of physical disability: Wheelchair use and public kindness. *The Sociological Quarterly, 36*(4), 681–698.

Carvalho D, T. S.-G.-C. (2013, October 17). The mirror neuron system in post-stroke rehabilitation. *International Archives of Medicine, 6*(41).

Caves, C.-R. (2019). *How contemporary Disney film can be used for mental health teaching in schools: A case study of Winnie the Pooh (2011) and Inside Out (2015)*. Retrieved from RC Psych: https://www.rcpsych.ac.uk/docs/default-source/members/divisions/london/london-essay-prizes/london-charlotte-caves-med-essay-prize-november-2020.pdf

Coleridge, S. T. (1817). *Biographia Literaria, Chapter XIV*. Retrieved from Poetry Foundation: https://www.poetryfoundation.org/articles/69385/from-biographia-literaria-chapter-xiv

Currys PC World. (2019). *Mental health and disabilities* (C. P. World, Producer) Retrieved from Diversity in Gaming: https://techtalk.currys.co.uk/tv-gaming/gaming/diversity-in-gaming/games-and-disabilities.html

Dewey, J. (1899). *The school and society, being three lectures*. Chicago, IL: University of Chicago Press.

Donaldson, M. (1978). *Children's minds*. Flamingo.

Egan, K. (1997). *The educated mind: How cognitive tools shape our understanding*. Chicago, IL: University of Chicago Press.

Engel, S. (1995). *The stories children tell*. New York, NY: Henry Holt and Co.

Feldman, H. M.-B. (2010, May). Diffusion tensor imaging: A review for pediatric researchers and clinicians. *Journal of Developmental and Behavioral Pediatrics, 31*(4), 346–356.

Fettes, M. (2010). The TIEs that bind: How imagination grasps the world. In K.S. Madej and K. Egan. (Eds.), *Understanding imagination and encouraging creativity in education*. Newcastle upon Tyne: Cambridge Scholars Press.

Fields, R. D. (2010, November 5). Change in the brain's white matter. *Science, 330*(6005), 768–769.

Freedberg, D. a. (2007). Movement, emotion and empathy in esthetic experience. *Trends in Cognitive Science, 11*(5), 197–203.

Gauvain, M., & Richert, R. (2022). *Cognitive development*. Retrieved from Neuroscience and Biobehavioral Psychology: https://www.sciencedirect.com/science/article/abs/pii/B9780323914970000485

Goering, S. (2015, June). Rethinking disability: The social model of disability and chronic disease. *Current Reviews in Musculoskeletal Medicine, 8*(2), 134–138.

Gogtay, N. J. (2004, May 17). Dynamic mapping of human cortical development during childhood through early adulthood. *PNAS, 101*(21), 8174–8179.

Gordon, A. (1995). *Star Wars*: A myth for our time. In A. Gordon (Ed.), *Screening the sacred*. New York, NY: Routledge.

Greenbaum, A. (2017, February 14). *Disabilities in video games are more realistic than you think.* Retrieved from Gamespresso!: https://www.gamespresso.com/2017/02/disabilities-video-games-realistic-think/

Gunter, B. (1998). *Effects of video games on children: The myth unmasked.* A&C Black.

Heilemann, F., Zimmermann, G., & Münster, P. (2021, October 20). Accessibility guidelines for VR games – A comparison and synthesis of a comprehensive set. *Frontiers in Virtual Reality, 20 October 2021 Sec. Technologies for VR Volume 2 – 2021 | https://doi.org/10.3389/frvir.2021.697504, 2.*

Henderson, M. S. (1997). *Star Wars: The magic of myth.* New York, NY: Bantam Spectra.

Huizinga, J. (1949). *Homo Ludens: A study of the play element in culture.* London: Kegan Paul Ltd.

——— (2019). *Is TV making your child prejudiced? A report into pre-school programming.* Hopster.

Jaclyn Packer, K. V. (2015, March–April). An overview of video description: History, benefits, and guidelines. *Journal of Visual Impairment & Blindness,* 83–93.

Jha, S. (2021, July). *Promoting inclusion and diversity in advertising.* Retrieved from Unicef.org: https://www.unicef.org/media/108811/file/UNICEF-PLAYBOOK-Promoting-diversity-and-inclusion-in-advertising.pdf

Johnson, M. a. (2021). *Normalizing mental illness and neurodiversity in entertainment media.* Milton Park: Routledge.

Kayhan, E. (2022, April). DEEP: A dual EEG pipeline for developmental hyperscanning studies. *Developmental Cognitive Neuroscience, 54.*

Kidd, K. (2004). Psychoanalysis and Children's Literature: The case for complementarity. *The Lion and the Unicorn,* 28.(1 (2004): 109–30; 28(a), 109–30.

Lack, C. (2023). *Major depressive disorder.* Retrieved from Abnormal Psychology: https://courses.lumenlearning.com/abnormalpsychology/chapter/major-depressive-disorder/

Learning Center. (2023). *Captioning timeline highlights.* Retrieved from The Described and Captioned Media Program: https://dcmp.org/learn/25

Ledder. (2020). On dis/ability within game studies. In R. G.-T. Ed. Katie Ellis (Ed.), *Interdisciplinary approaches to disability looking towards the future: Volume 2* (Vol. 2). New York, NY: Routledge.

Lott, C. (2021). *History of closed captions: The analog era.* Retrieved from Hackaday: https://hackaday.com/2021/04/14/history-of-closed-captions-the-analog-era/

MacDonald, J. F., Marsden, M. T., & Geist, C. D. (1980). Radio and television studies and American culture. *American Quarterly, 32*(3), 301–317.

Madej, K. (2007). *Connecting print and digital game.* Burnaby, BC: Simon Fraser University.

Madej, K. (2016). *Physical play and Children's digital games.* Switzerland: Springer Nature.

Madej, K. (2017). *Taking on serious topics in children's entertainment games.* Retrieved from Computers in Entertainment: https://cie.acm.org

Madej, K. (2018, April). *Children's games, from Turtle to Squirtle.* (N. Lee, Ed.). Retrieved from Encyclopedia of Computer Graphics and Games: https://link.springer.com/content/pdf/10.1007/978-3-319-08234-9_103-2.pdf

Madigan, S., Eirich, R., Pador, P., McArthur, B., & Neville, R. (2022). Assessment of changes in child and adolescent screen time during the COVID-19 pandemic: A systematic review and meta-analysis. *JAMA Pediatrics, 176*(12), 1188–1198.

McVee, M. B., Dunsmore, K., & James, J. R. (2005, Winter). Schema theory revisited. *Review of Educational Research, 75*(4), 531–566.

Media Smarts. (2022). Common portrayals of persons with disabilities. Retrieved from Media Smarts: https://mediasmarts.ca/diversity-media/persons-disabilities/common-portrayals-persons-disabilities

Miranda, F. (2015). *Approach – EEP assessment.* Retrieved from Bright Minds Institute: http://www.brightmindsinstitute.com

Morita, T. A. (2016, September 15). Contribution of neuroimaging studies to understanding development of human cognitive brain functions. *Frontiers in Human Neuroscience, 10.*

NIA. (2023). *What is dementia? Symptoms, types, and diagnosis.* Retrieved from National Institute on Aging: https://www.nia.nih.gov/health/what-is-dementia

Oliver, M. (1996). *Understanding disability: From theory to practice.* New York, NY: St. Martin's Press.

Orland, K. (2013, March 4). *Auti-sim lets you experience the horror of sensory overload.* Retrieved from Ars Technica: https://arstechnica.com/gaming/2013/03/auti-sim-lets-you-experience-the-horror-of-sensory-overload/

Parlock, J. (2020, January 8). *Video games and disability: Looking back at a challenging decade.* Retrieved from Polygon: https://www.polygon.com/2020/1/8/21056713/disabilities-video-game-characters-inclusion-accessibility-decade-in-review

Piaget, J. (1972). *The psychology of the child.* New York, NY: Basic Books.

Plato. (380 B.C.E). *The Republic.* Retrieved from http://classics.mit.edu/Plato/republic.html

Porter, B. (2020). *Finding Dory's memories: The neuroscience behind Disney Pixar's Finding Dory.* Retrieved from Dr. Blake Porter: https://www.blakeporterneuro.com/finding-dorys-memories-the-neuroscience-behind-disney-pixars-finding-dory/

Pratte, W. (2021, August 17). *Geoffrey Goes to the Fair.* (K. Madej, Interviewer).

Qiu, A. M. (2015, January). Diffusion tensor imaging for understanding brain development in early life. *Annual Review of Psychology, 66*, 853–876.

Resene, M. (2017, Spring). From evil queen to disabled teen: Frozen introduces Disney's first disabled princess. *Disability Studies Quarterly, 37*(2).

Rosen, B. (2011). *fMRI at 20: Has it changed the world?* Retrieved from Athinoula A. Martinos Center for Biomedical Imaging: https://www.nmr.mgh.harvard.edu/history/fmri-at-20

Salen, K., & Zimmerman, E. (2003). *Rules of play: Game design fundamentals.* Cambridge, MA: MIT Press.

Sarge, M. A.-S., Kim, H.-S., & Velez, J. A. (2020, January 21). An auti-sim intervention: The role of perspective taking in combating public stigma with virtual simulations. *Cyberpsychology, Behavior, and Social Networking,* 41–51.

Schank, R. C. (1990). *Tell me a story: Narrative and intelligence.* Evanston, IL: Northwestern University Press.

Schweik, S. M. (2009). *The ugly laws: Disability in public.* New York, NY: NYU Press.

Shea, S. E. (2000, December 12). Pathology in the Hundred Acre Wood: A neurodevelopmental perspective on A.A. Milne. *CMAJ, 163*(12), 1557–1559.

Shell, J. (2021, March 13). What do we see: An investigation into the representation of disability in video games. *arXiv:2103.17100.*

Sherer, T. (2020, August 3). *Video game representation.* Retrieved from New Mobility: https://newmobility.com/video-game-representation/

Sisk, C. F. (2004, October). The neural basis of puberty and adolescence. *Nature Neuroscience, 7,* 1040–1047.

Smedley, T. (2015, July 11). *Children's TV pretends disability doesn't exist.* Retrieved from Guardian Sustainable Business: https://www.theguardian.com/sustainable-business/2015/jul/28/childrens-tv-representation-disability-nickelodoen-disney-bbc

Sowell, E. P. (2003, March). Mapping cortical change across the human life span. *Nature Neuroscience, 6,* 309–315.

Sullivan, P. (2015, November 1). *Pulse review – A great idea blinded by poor mechanics.* Retrieved from Cog Connected: https://cogconnected.com/review/pulse-review-a-great-idea-blinded-by-poor-mechanics/

Switzer, J. (2003). *Disabled rights: American disability policy and the fight for equality.* Washington, DC: Georgetown University Press.

Sylwester, R. (1995). *A celebration of neurons: An educator's guide to the human brain.* Alexandria, VA: Association for Supervision and Curriculum Development.

Taylor, S. E. (1989). *Positive illusions: Creative self-deception and the healthy mind.* New York, NY: Basic Books.

Thompson, C. (2019, March). *GDC showcase: You can take an arrow to the knee and still be an adventurer.* Retrieved from YouTube: https://www.youtube.com/watch?v=Vb39BFs1UK0&t=1s

Thomsen, M. (2014, November 19). *Ether One: The video game that tries to simulate dementia.* Retrieved from New Yorker: https://www.newyorker.com/business/currency/ether-one-video-game-tries-simulate-dementia

Tomasello, M. (2021). *Becoming human.* Cambridge, MA: Harvard University Press.

Tucker, D., & Luu, P. (2012). *Cognition and neural development.* New York, NY: Oxford University Press.

Ventä-Olkkonen, L. a.-J.-C. (2021). CHI against bullying: Taking stock of the past and envisioning the future. *DIS '21: Designing Interactive Systems,* pp. 734–748.

Vygotsky, L. (1978). *Mind in society: The development of higher psychological processes.* Cambridge, MA: Harvard University Press.

Wagoner, B. (2017). Frederic Bartlett. In *Handbook of the philosophy of memory.* Routledge.

Watters, A. (2015, February 25). *How Steve Jobs brought the apple II to the classroom.* Retrieved from Hack Education: http://hackeducation.com/2015/02/25/kids-cant-wait-apple

Watts, J. (2019, March 11). *Greta Thunberg, schoolgirl climate change warrior: 'Some people can let things go. I can't'.* Retrieved from The Guardian: https://www.theguardian.com/world/2019/mar/11/greta-thunberg-schoolgirl-climate-change-warrior-some-people-can-let-things-go-i-cant

What Is Culture? (2023). Retrieved from CARLA: https://carla.umn.edu/culture/definitions.html

Whitebread, D. (2012, April). The importance of play: A report on the value of children's play with a series of policy recommendations. Toy Industries of Europe.

WHO. (2013). *How to use the ICF: A practical manual for using the international classification of functioning, disability and health (ICF).* World Health Organization. Geneva: World Health Organization.

Wicas, G. (2013, January 31). *Neuropsychological review life moment to moment: Memento as a case study in anterograde amnesia.* Retrieved from NeuroPsyFi: https://www.neuropsyfi.com/reviews/memento

Wilds, S. (2020, January). *For all the players: A history of accessibility in video games.* Retrieved from Gaming Bible: https://www.gamingbible.com/features/games-for-all-the-players-a-history-of-accessibility-in-video-games-20200124

Winnicott, D. (1971). *Playing and reality.* London: Tavistock Publications.

Wolf, M. J. (2015). *Video games around the world.* Cambridge, MA: MIT Press.

Wood, D. (1998). *How children think and learn* (2nd ed.). Oxford, UK: Blackwell Publishers.

Young, R. M. (2005, May 28). *Melanie Klein I.* (I. P. Young, Producer) Retrieved Mar 15, 2016, from The Human Nature Review: http://human-nature.com/rmyoung/papers/pap127h.html

Yuan, B., Folmer, E., & Harris, F. C. Jr. (2010, June 25). Game accessibility: A survey. *Universal Access in the Information Society Volume, 10,* 81–100.

Zallio, M., & Ohashi, T. (2022). The evolution of assistive technology: A literature review of technology developments and applications. *Preprint of AHFE international conference, 2022.*

Index

.